JESSICA HOWE

KINKY SEX

THE SECRET TO LONG-TERM DESIRE

Website: www.thekinkysexbook.com

Facebook and Twitter: TheKinkySexBook

Email: contact@thekinkysexbook.com

ISBN: 978-0-9775524-1-2

Ebook ISBN: 978-0-9775524-2-9

ACKNOWLEDGEMENTS

Many amazing people made this book possible. I'm particularly grateful to the hundreds of courageous individuals who gave up their deepest, darkest sex secrets and fantasies when I interviewed them. Their names are changed, but their experiences remain refreshingly, honestly and candidly shared on these pages.

Thanks to Sophie Morgan, best-selling author of *The Diary of a Submissive*, for her encouragement from all the way across the world, and to sex experts Tracey Cox, Jacqueline Hellyer, Dr. Pamela Stephenson Connolly and Jack Morin for their world-leading expertise and insight.

A big pat on the back to talented photographer and friend Malcolm Grant for making me look good in the cover photo. Also to model and friend Kedori for his masterful grip on that chain – and for calming my pre-shoot nerves with my favourite Pinot Grigio.

I'm grateful to the talented Haki Crisden for his kinkalicious editing and wholehearted dedication – and for being, as he promised, totally and delightfully unshockable! Thanks go to Alex the Grecian god for the book jacket design and Mark Laverty for his sex-pectacular illustrations. Also to Lee and JP at Buzz Web Media for their creativity and enthusiasm, and for going the extra mile.

Thank you to Savannah, Andrew, Peta, John, Stewart and Matt for welcoming me into their homes when times were tough during this book's creation. Also to Sharon, who read the very first draft and gave me the expert feedback I so needed.

I'm grateful to Jeff Gilling who, just weeks before publication, swooped in like an angel to make a big splash, and to rakish rogue Charles Waterstreet, for backing *Kinky Sex* without batting an eyelid. Huge thanks also to my dear friends Tim, Lucas, Antonia, Andy, Greco, Stewart, Ailsa, Craig, Peta and Lauren for cheering me on and believing in me every step of the way. Whenever I doubted the sanity of writing such a book, they were there to support me and spur me on.

But most of all, thank you to my readers, especially those of you who take the time to write to me. I look forward to your emails, Facebook posts, blog comments and Amazon reviews as much as I do to a well-delivered OTK spanking.

Well, almost.

Sex is part of nature. I go along with nature.

– Marilyn Monroe

The only way of full knowledge lies in the act of love; this act transcends thought, it transcends words. It is the daring plunge into the experience of union.

– Erich Fromm

Twenty years from now you will be more disappointed by the things that you didn't do than by the ones you did do. So throw off the bowlines. Sail away from the safe harbor. Catch the trade winds in your sails. Explore. Dream. Discover.

– Mark Twain

CONTENTS

Why You Need to Read This Book 11

•••

PART I – GETTING INTO IT

Read This First 16

CHAPTER 1

The Top Six Passion Assassins 17

    1. Too close for sex 17

    2. Complacency 20

    3. Masturbating into your lover 22

    4. Sex versus sleaze 23

    5. 'Good Girl' and 'Good Guy' Syndrome 24

    6. But they'll freak out! 27

CHAPTER 2

Discover Your Secret Sexual Personality 31

    The sexual personality quiz 32

    Results and what they mean 34

CHAPTER 3

How to Find a Sexually Compatible Lover 41

    Where do I go to meet kinky people? 43

    Discover someone's secret sexual personality 43

Attract the right lover with hints and signals 45

When should I bring it up?.. 47

How to meet a kinky partner online........................ 48

When and how to broach kinky sex with a
potential partner... 51

CHAPTER 4

How to Get Your Lover into Kinky Sex........................ 55

What if my lover's only ever experienced
vanilla sex? 55

Bringing up your fantasies without risking
rejection 56

Connect more deeply with your lover...................... 58

Discover your lover's secret fantasies and
how to push their hot buttons 60

Turn your lover on with dirty talk 62

Turn your fantasies into fact 68

CHAPTER 5

How to Heighten Your Sexual Chemistry................... 71

Where do I start?... 71

Set the scene for seduction....................................... 73

How to become irresistible to your lover 75

The Lovers' List.. 77

The one technique that makes sex hotter
every time 79

•••

PART II – GETTING IT ON

CHAPTER 6
Sensation Play 87

CHAPTER 7
The Science of Spanking 107

CHAPTER 8
Frisky and Risky: Public Play 125

CHAPTER 9
Domination/submission 139

CHAPTER 10
Bondage for Beginners 173

CHAPTER 11
Role Play 195

CHAPTER 12
Ladies First: Femdom 209

CHAPTER 13
Anal Adventures 225

•••

PART III – GETTING GEARED UP

CHAPTER 14
The Free Sex Toys All Around Your Home 243

CHAPTER 15

Create Your Own Sex Toy Kit..249

EPILOGUE

Where To From Here? 255

WHY YOU NEED TO READ THIS BOOK

It's possible to live on bread and water. Perhaps not desirable, but you won't starve.

Bread and water are the food equivalent of mainstream sex: filling and thirst-quenching but not terribly exciting. And however fancy the focaccia bread or sparkling the mineral water, it's still, well, just bread and water.

And if that's all you've ever tasted, you're in for a treat – or should I say, a series of treats. Because just a few page turns from now you'll be smack, bang in the middle of a feast of decadent delicacies, each more tempting than the last.

But that nine-course degustation might look a little intimidating to you right now. Which bits of cutlery do you use for what? And how do you decide what to try first?

Alternatively, perhaps you have a highly charged erotic imagination but haven't yet dared to use it. If so, I'm about to help you come out from hiding. Because as you'll soon see, you secretly harbour the ambrosia that keeps relationships sizzlingly sexy, vibrant and explorative. And whether you're carefree and single or married with children, you'll discover how to live out your frisky fantasies without being called a freak.

The seeds of this book were sown at an unexpectedly dark time in my life, just after the 2006 launch of my first book, *The One Stop Wedding Kit.* As it flew up Amazon's bestseller lists and wedding magazines sang its praises, ironically my own marriage, after 14 years, was disintegrating.

Sexual incompatibility was tearing us apart. I learned the hard way that, contrary to conventional thinking, if a relationship is based on love the sex part doesn't 'just work'. Faced with the painful conclusion that a marriage without sex is just a friendship, we divorced.

So I began soul-searching. What went wrong? How could I prevent it from ever happening again? And most importantly, how could I find and nurture a relationship that would stay exciting, sexy and interesting?

This book is the culmination of seven years I spent on both sides of the globe in a quest to find answers to those questions. My experiences, and the stories people so generously shared with me, form the heart of this book. They revealed that exploring your kinky sides creates an unquenchable thirst for each other, a passionate craving. You never run out of things to try because opening one door just presents you with three more exciting choices, and each time, you're hanging to turn the handle. Exploring the maze together is heady, thrilling and deeply bonding.

Best of all, I discovered the secret, magical ingredient to fuelling long-term desire, which I'll be sharing with you here on every page. It involves stimulating the most erogenous part of the body: the mind.

And this is great news, because it means you don't have to look like a heartbreakingly handsome Spanish movie star or a Swedish supermodel to have mind-bending, fantastic, deeply intimate, connected, multi-orgasmic sex! You just need to develop your erotic inspiration – and fortunately, with the techniques in this book, that's easy.

So do you need to work at the sex? I believe it's more important to *play* at the sex, and that means seeing it as an ongoing adventure you're on together. Variety enriches life, but to know what turns you and your lover on you'll need to experiment. Each time you discover something new about yourself you'll have one more pleasure-enhancing way of connecting to add to your repertoire. It's a great way to keep your love life fresh.

Your body and mind were created with the ability to experience all sorts of erotic pleasure, so why not delight in it? I'm here to tell you that your sexual potential is your birthright, and to take you by the hand to begin exploring its limitless possibilities.

PART I
GETTING INTO IT

READ THIS FIRST!

Always remember to be respectful of each other and use your common sense. In particular, keep your play:

Consensual – The line between fun, kinky sex and outright abuse is one word: consent. Whatever activity from this book you engage in, make sure you do it with the full consent of your partner. That means

- Never pressure someone into doing something they don't want to do.
- Check in with your partner throughout play to confirm that they still consent.
- Always play with a safeword. This is something you wouldn't typically say, like 'red', which when used by either partner immediately calls a halt to play.

Safe – Don't try anything that's unsafe or likely to get you injured or harmed, inform yourself of the dos and don'ts so you can perform any activity without injury, and practise safe sex. Ensure the emotional safety of yourself and your lover, and clearly communicate your needs and wants.

Sane – Make sure you are both in a rational state of mind when you play. Know the difference between fantasy and reality, and don't play when you're impaired by drugs or alcohol.

CHAPTER 1

....

THE TOP SIX PASSION ASSASSINS

"It just fizzled out." "Things went flat." "The spark's gone." It's the ultimate modern mystery: why do so many once fun, exciting relationships nosedive into the Friend Zone? And what can you do to stop it happening to yours?

We typically blame loss of desire on raising young children, financial stress, long working hours or family commitments. But however real these obstacles are, the true culprits lie elsewhere. In this chapter you'll discover the top six passion assassins and what you can do to safely disarm them.

1. TOO CLOSE FOR SEX

When you've been with someone for a while, sex is rarely as wild and exciting as it was in the early days. You develop a routine. You know exactly how to bring your lover to orgasm quickly and efficiently, and they know just how to return the favour. It gets the job done but before long that same old set of moves gets boring. That's when many of us begin to lose interest and look elsewhere.

So what's the solution? For a long time we've been told that increasing emotional intimacy will fix everything, but more and more sex therapists are questioning this.

Many couples get emotionally intimate, as I did with my ex-husband, but their sex lives plummet anyway. Awesome sex requires two vital elements: trust and lust. And whilst long-term relationships increase our trust, our lust for each other tends to dwindle.

A number of experts now believe that emotional intimacy makes us best friends rather than lusty lovers. The very same closeness that makes us feel comfortable and safe with each other actually drives us apart sexually. We become so close that we do everything together, and as we lose our sense of identity our sexual interest in each other wanes. After all, who wants to have sex with themselves?

According to Jack Morin, world-leading expert on the intimacy-versus-sex enigma, we find separateness more attractive than similarity. To be turned on by someone we need to see them as an individual with their own interests, opinions and personality. Conflict and opposition can actually stimulate desire.

According to Morin's research, couples who have the best sex are differentiated: they have different tastes and ideas and realise they'll never truly know each other. They have less in common than many couples that seem idyllic, complementing each other rather than merging into one.

Each pushes the other forward into uncharted territory, challenging them to grow and experiment. And whilst this is important in every part of life, nowhere is it more vital than in the area of sex.

"Sexual curiosity is a fairly common reason why some people choose to stray," says Dr Pamela Stephenson Connolly, best-selling author of *Sex Life*. That's because we find novelty arousing. Supply sexual novelty within the relationship and you build a strong foundation; let things atrophy and it's likely that you or your partner will find that novelty in a new lover.

A growing number of experts now believe that challenging and pushing each other's boundaries sexually is, in fact, the key to keeping the passion alive. After all, when it comes to novelty, conventional sex has only a limited number of first times (first kiss, first oral sex, first intercourse) whilst kinky sex offers us an unlimited array of them.

Non-consensual celibacy

Conventional wisdom says that if one partner doesn't want sex the other should tolerate this, stick out the relationship and stay monogamous. I call this 'non-consensual celibacy' and in my opinion, it's unreasonable, unfair and often leads to infidelity.

It's rare for both partners to be happy in a low- or no-sex relationship: usually one wants sex, even if the other doesn't. It's time for us to stop mud-slinging and admit affairs are not random events – that both partners share responsibility for allowing the relationship to stagnate. The bottom line is, stop having sex with each other and the chances are that one or both of you will end up having sex with someone else.

---

2. COMPLACENCY

For most of us, the feeling of being desired is a far greater turn-on than emotional intimacy. That's why when you stop feeling wanted by your partner, that hot stranger who's flirting with you at the bar suddenly becomes so tempting.

When was the last time you told your lover how sexy they are? Many of us do this frequently at the start of a relationship but less as time goes on, when the routine of loading the dishwasher, paying the bills and seeing the in-laws kicks in. Before we know it we're trading our Agent Provocateur lingerie for a comfy pair of tracksuit pants, cuddling up in front of the TV rather than surfing online for new sex toys.

The thing is, *we tend to feel desire for people who desire us.* This is why so many people have affairs. They no longer feel desired at home, so when they meet someone who wants them and finds them attractive, they succumb.

You can make your lover feel wanted by embracing whatever it is that makes you both feel fun, young and sexy. You might think more money will make you happier, but according to research by American economists David Blanchflower and Andrew Oswald, having a lasting marriage and frequent sex is the equivalent of getting a $100,000 pay rise. Invest in that occasional dirty weekend away and you could just be saving your relationship.

Feed desire by showing appreciation for your lover. Go beyond the catch-all "you're beautiful" and compliment all the many nuances that make them exciting to you. Saying "you look so sexy when you're sleepy" or "your accent drives me wild" sends the message that you don't just theoretically admire their beauty from afar, you notice myriad things about them that make you really want to get down and dirty.

How to make your man feel sexy

Men are often adept at courting women with compliments on their appearance, but they rarely receive them. Whispering into his ear, "You look so hot in that suit, I can't wait for you to spank me in it," as you both leave for the office puts thoughts of what's to come in his head all day long. Desire is simply un-fulfilled erotic anticipation, so teasing works wonders.

Tell him his bum looks great in those jeans or how sexy and strong his arms are. Saying he's a great kisser or gives you mind-blowing oral sex will seriously boost his ego, since men tend to be performance driven.

The pièce de résistance? Say you just *love* the way he's so open to trying new things – unlike your last boyfriend. Before you know it you'll have him swinging from the chandeliers!

Kinky sex is, in essence, all about demonstrating your desire for your lover. It's about showing you're so crazy about them that you want to take them to places they've never been, to spark that electricity between you, to give them incredible experiences. To let down your barriers and trust, to make what you have between you unlike anything they've ever had – or ever could have – with anyone else.

If you do all that, do you really think they'll be looking elsewhere?

3. MASTURBATING INTO YOUR LOVER

We all carry the heavy burden of our past programming. As Australian sex therapist Jacqueline Hellyer points out, for millennia we've been raising our girl children to think being sexual is wrong, sending them to asylums or stoning them to death if they indulge their curiosity. With no opportunity to explore their own erotic nature, when women married they couldn't tell men how to please them.

On the other hand, as Hellyer puts it, "Since puberty the adolescent boy had been stroking his penis as fast as he could until he ejaculated. So when he got a female partner, not knowing any better, he kept doing that inside her. Essentially men were masturbating inside their wives." Hellyer calls this the Adolescent Male Masturbatory Model.

With the realisation that less than 30% of women can orgasm through penetrative sex alone, most men now know women's bodies usually need to be stimulated in some other way to reach orgasm. This led to what Hellyer describes as the *Chivalrous* Adolescent Male Masturbatory Model.

"That is," she explains, "give her an orgasm first, and then masturbate into her. There's still an expectation that they'll both be horny first, that the genitals are the focus, the orgasm is the main event, and it's all over when he comes. Boring!"

Sound familiar? In contrast, kinky sex is a journey in itself — not a five-second orgasmic ending. How to take yourself and your lover on that journey is what this book is all about.

4. SEX VERSUS SLEAZE

Unfortunately, most of us associate sex with sleaze rather than eroticism and sensuality. This notion comes from the 1970s, when our long-repressed sexuality was unleashed in male-focused, immature and fairly sordid representations. One of the biggest expressions of this was porn, much of which continues today to show women in various degrading situations.

Most women like to be respected by their partner, not degraded, so it's hardly surprising that they don't want to be seen as porn stars. And understandably, most men have far too much respect for their girlfriends or wives to want to see them or treat them as such.

As you can see, the sex = porn cliché is a real barrier to experimentation. Nowhere is this more prevalent than the area of kinky sex. But in reality, porn has about as much to do with kinky sex as the children's fairy tale *The Little Mermaid* has to do with deep-sea fishing. For example:

- Porn shows nothing of intimacy and connection; kinky sex is *all* about intimacy and connection.
- Porn is purely visual titillation; kink is about touch and sensuality.
- In porn, the camera focuses on the point of entry, and since touching obscures the view there's little or no other bodily contact; in kinky sex there's plenty of yummy skin-on-skin, stroking and closeness.
- In porn, women get instantly turned on just by the presence of a man; in reality, women need an erotic lead-up, flirtation or seduction to become aroused.

- Porn shows lots of genital friction resulting in an orgasm; kinky sex is about getting into each other's heads and taking your lover on a bliss-filled journey.

I'm not saying porn is inherently bad, but it's entirely different from real-life sex. Porn is there to titillate, not educate, as the ground-breaking site makelovenotporn.com shows. Because it's a purely visual medium, porn can never even scratch the surface of how mind-blowingly intimate and profoundly bonding sex can be.

As an aside, it's no coincidence that porn often prevents sexual communication between couples. Its unrealistic scenes and addictive qualities keep people coming back for more, instead of talking to their partners about what they want.

5. 'GOOD GIRL' AND 'GOOD GUY' SYNDROME

At the other end of the spectrum from "sex = sleaze" is what I call Good Girl/Good Guy Syndrome – and it's just as destructive. Seeing yourself as a Good Girl can stop you exploring the fantasies that turn you on and the wonderful world of pleasures you're capable of experiencing.

What's a scene?

It's a defined period of sexually charged play that may or may not include penetrative sex. During a scene you may choose to indulge in consensual erotic power exchange (see the chapter on Domination/submission), perhaps putting aside your everyday personas and indulging in spanking, bondage, acts of service, etc. A scene may last as little as an hour or for a day or more.

We all come with our own pre-conceived ideas of what sex is, what's OK to do, what's OK to ask for and what's just plain taboo. Most of the time those ideas are fuzzy and ill-defined and we seldom compare notes with our lover.

You might feel guilty or fearful of being judged as slutty for talking about the things you fantasise about. Taken to the extreme, this way of thinking leaves you in a place where you have problems seeing yourself as a sexual person.

Equally damaging but less often recognised is the man who sees himself as a Good Guy and has very clear ideas about what women want and how he should treat them. Preconceptions like these can stop you from focusing on your lover and what she *really* wants.

Take your Good Guy persona too far and you'll find yourself putting your lady on such a high pedestal that you no longer see her as sexual. Blindsided by the traditional ethos that love is good but lust is bad, you could find yourself loving, but not desiring your partner – and instead, fulfilling your sexual needs by indulging the 'sinful' part of you with prostitutes, porn or casual pick-ups.

However, your lover is sexual, and she wants you to find her sexy. We all like to feel desired, especially by our partner! The reality is that each woman is unique, with different turn-ons, her body and mind unexplored territory. So focus on discovering what the woman you're with *actually* wants, and then on giving it to her.

Remove any notion of 'what women are meant to want' and accept that men and women are capable of all sorts of dirty, delicious desires and fantasies. Once you do that, you're much closer to opening up an honest conversation without judgement about what turns each of you on. And the only way to do that is to make each other feel safe talking about it, which we'll explore in Chapter 3.

There is nothing inherently bad about sex, including kinky sex. The question to ask is, does what you're doing or what you want to do help you and your lover grow and flourish? Is it something that enhances your connection?

Converted to kink?

The phone rang just as I was writing this and it was my friend Dave. He's always claimed to enjoy only vanilla sex, and though he doesn't judge me for my kinky inclinations he has always found them rather strange and amusing.

Today, however, he couldn't wait to tell me about a recent encounter at an event he attended after a cricket match. Everyone was given mini cricket bats and he and his girlfriend began playfully slapping each other on the backside. He was totally unprepared for the way his body responded.

"I've never felt anything like it, Jess. It felt incredible – I haven't been that turned on for ages! I've never even thought of doing stuff like that. I mean I thought you were kind of crazy with all this kinky stuff. But now I really get it!"

As you can see, even lovers of very conventional sex can find themselves inexplicably and profoundly turned on when they try a little kink in a low-pressure context. So welcome to the Dark Side, Dave – I'm happy I helped you see the light!

6. BUT THEY'LL FREAK OUT!

It's a conundrum: if you're in a casual relationship you can be as kinky as you like because you don't really care if you're rejected, but in a committed relationship there's just too much fallout if your lover judges you harshly. So you begin to self-censor. "Will he think I'm a freak if I suggest tying him up?" "Will she think I'm a misogynist if I want to call her names in bed?"

Even couples who've been married for decades can be too afraid to confess their desires to each other. Sadly, many of them probably fantasise about trying the same things, but they don't voice their wishes because they risk losing each other.

Many people are so terrified of asking their partners for what they want that they end up indulging themselves with strangers, staying proper and restrained at home. Before you know it, there's a chasm between you that's so wide it's no longer possible for either of you to bridge it.

But it's OK to suggest doing delectably deviant things to your lover. Whatever it is you'd like to try it's probably not as unusual as you think, and you don't need to apologise for wanting a vibrant, fun, explorative sex life.

Scared of the reaction you'll get? If you've never asked your lover if they'd be interested in explorative sex, you just can't know how they'll respond. Sex can be a tricky topic to raise so be wary of jumping to conclusions just because your lover hasn't told you they'd like to experiment. I'll be showing you step-by-step how to introduce kinky sex into your relationship without risking rejection in Chapter 4.

WHERE TO FROM HERE?

If you're attached, begin to conquer the passion assassins by opening up conversations that question conventional wisdom about sex, comparing notes on how you both feel society represents sex and what influence that's had on you both.

Here are some conversation starters to get your lover thinking and questioning the status quo. If you need a lead-in, say you read a magazine article or saw a TV programme about the topic and are intrigued to hear their opinion.

- What do you think the difference is between love and lust? Do you think most relationships have both, or just one?
- When you think of the word 'slut', do you see it as good or bad? How do you define a slut – as a woman with a healthy sexual appetite who likes to experiment with one person, or a woman who sleeps around?
- What do you think young people learn about sex from porn? In what ways does it help and in what ways does it harm their sexual identity?
- How do you think porn influences men's and women's sexual expectations and experiences?
- Can sex be wild and experimental without being sordid and sleazy?
- If something is forbidden or transgressive, is it more sexy?
- Do you think someone can know if they'll like something sexual without having tried it?
- How do you think people maintain the sexual spark in a long-term relationship?

- Do you think couples who share everything have better sex, or is there something to be said for maintaining some mystery?

Questions like these about sex and society are less confronting than, for example, "What are you into?" Once your partner sees your goal is to deepen your sexual connection, you're ready to open up more personal topics, which we'll be talking about in Chapter 4.

Remember, there's no jury sitting in your bedroom passing judgement on you for what's acceptable and what's not. A sexual activity that's freaky to one person can be standard for another. The only people who get to decide what to do and what not to do are you and your lover.

Sex is the one and only thing you get to do with your lover and no one else. Not only does it feel great physically, it makes us feel desired, admired, close and connected. But what exactly are you into? Without trying something it can be hard to know.

In the next chapter we'll be looking at what makes you tick sexually, and how to use that understanding to inspire the best sex of your life.

CHAPTER 2

DISCOVER YOUR SECRET SEXUAL PERSONALITY

What are your hot buttons? Without having tried something, often it's hard to know if you'll like it, so this chapter is dedicated to helping you understand the cues that turn you on with a little quiz.

If you're single, understanding this gives you clues about the type of person you might find sexually compatible. If you're in a relationship, taking the quiz separately and then comparing answers gives you a deeper level of appreciation for each other's turn-ons.

Prepare yourself for surprises that will springboard you to a greatly enhanced sex life. Your lover's a voyeur and you're not? Then visually titillate them by wearing that low-cut dress they love, text them a sexy photo of yourself or bring a full-length mirror into the bedroom. Knowing your partner's secret sexual personality is the magic key that unlocks a whole new world of interactions.

Answer these questions according to your feelings and behaviour in a sexual context, not a social one. If there's something you haven't tried, ask yourself whether the idea of doing it appeals to you. And take the results with a pinch of salt – this won't give you all the answers but it's a great place to start!

THE SEXUAL PERSONALITY QUIZ

1. I think sexual experimentation is an important part of a healthy relationship. Yes / No

2. I like to feel powerful and in control during sex play. Yes / No

3. Sexual situations in which I am physically restrained are exciting. Yes / No

4. I like taking orders from my lover and pleasing them in whatever way they tell me to. Yes / No

5. I'd like to explore my lover's sexual fantasies. Yes / No

6. I would enjoy posing for my lover naked. Yes / No

7. I enjoy tying my partner up. Yes / No

8. I often fantasise about having sex in public. Yes / No

9. I would like to watch people have sex. Yes / No

10. I like to say things during sex that make my partner uncomfortable. Yes / No

11. I'm turned on by the idea of my lover watching me undress. Yes / No

12. Trying different sexual things is what keeps the spark in a relationship. Yes / No

13. Being tied up makes me feel safe. Yes / No

14. I enjoy the idea of being overpowered during sex. Yes / No

15. I like spanking my lover. Yes / No

16. I enjoy watching pornography. Yes / No

17. I often fantasise about tying my lover up.   Yes / No

18. Seeing my lover's eagerness to sexually serve me is hot.   Yes / No

19. Sexual experimentation's not for me, I'm happy with how things are.   Yes / No

20. I love the idea of being punished.   Yes / No

21. I love to watch my partner and I have sex in a mirror.   Yes / No

22. I'm aroused by the idea of calling my lover dirty names during sex play.   Yes / No

23. I like the feeling of being pinned down or having my hair pulled.   Yes / No

24. I like to take pictures of my lover naked.   Yes / No

25. I want to continue doing what I know turns me on rather than trying anything new.   Yes / No

26. The fantasy of participating in an orgy appeals to me.   Yes / No

27. Sometimes I like to take control sexually and other times I like to give up control.   Yes / No

28. I like the feeling or the idea of having my wrists tied.   Yes / No

29. I am aroused by the idea of people watching me have sex.   Yes / No

30. It's exciting when my lover willingly gives up control to me.   Yes / No

31. I like watching my lover undress.   Yes / No

32. I prefer to change sexual roles depending on how I feel.   Yes / No

33. I would love to be restrained during sex.   Yes / No

34. Sex toys take away from the intimacy between my partner and I.   Yes / No

35. I would love to film my lover and I having sex.   Yes / No

36. It would be interesting to try things that are out of my normal sexual range.   Yes / No

37. It turns me on to be called names during sex.   Yes / No

38. So far as I know, I don't have any fetishes.   Yes / No

39. I like the idea of being dominant sometimes, and submissive at others.   Yes / No

40. I like the idea of physically restraining my lover.   Yes / No

41. I think sexual experimentation would bring me closer to my lover.   Yes / No

Results and what they mean	Your score
Count up how many 'yes' answers you gave for questions 6, 8, 11, 26 and 29. If you have 3 or more 'yes' answers, you have a strong inclination towards **Exhibitionism**.	

Count up how many 'yes' answers you gave for questions 9, 16, 21, 24, 31 and 35. If you have 3 or more 'yes' answers, you incline towards **Voyeurism**.	
Count up how many 'yes' answers you gave for questions 2, 10, 15, 18, 22 and 30. If you have 3 or more 'yes' answers, you are turned on by being in a role of **Dominance**.	
Count up how many 'yes' answers you gave for questions 4, 14, 20, 23, 33 and 37. If you have 3 or more 'yes' answers, you're drawn towards a role of **Submission**.	
Count up how many 'yes' answers you gave for questions 27, 32 and 39. If you answered 'yes' to 2 or more of these, you enjoy both dominating and submitting, which means you enjoy **Switching**.	
Add up how many 'yes' answers you gave for questions 3, 7, 13, 17, 28 and 40. If you have 2 or more 'yes' answers, you like **Bondage**.	
Count up how many 'yes' answers you gave for questions 1, 5, 12, 36 and 41. Then count up how many 'yes' answers you have for questions 19, 25, 34 and 38 and deduct this from your figure. If you have three or more 'yes' answers, you like to experiment and are pretty **Kinky**.	

The exhibitionist

Get a kick from the idea of being caught in the act? Maybe you've had sex outdoors, played around in the back seat of a taxi, worn revealing clothing or gone skinny dipping? The impulse to show off is in most of us if we're honest, so it's not surprising that exhibitionism is such a popular fantasy for both men and women. It's also the one we're most likely to act out.

Within a consensual, adult relationship, exhibitionism is normal and fun. The appeal lies in the power that we feel from arousing those who are observing us and the thrill of possibly being caught.

If you scored high on exhibitionism and your lover's a voyeur, lucky you! There's endless fun to be had and the section on Public Play (Chapter 8) gives you plenty of ideas.

The voyeur

Do you enjoy watching your lover undress, behave sexually or wear revealing clothing? Perhaps you like the idea of having sex as you look in a mirror, or videoing the experience?

As a voyeur, you may be turned on by your partner playfully flashing you in public. It's usually a passive role, but some voyeurs like to dominate by directing their lover's performance.

You don't have to like porn and strip shows to be a voyeur; most of us like to watch to some extent. Both men and women rate visual cues highly in choosing a partner, we love people watching and we're suckers for reality TV shows. It's only a problem if it's done non-consensually: peeping toms are not well liked! As a voyeur, you're perfectly suited to an exhibitionistic partner and again, you'll love the chapter on Public Play.

The Dominant ('Dom' if male, 'Domme' if female)

Have you fantasised about telling your lover exactly what to do and having her obey your every word? Or pinning him down to have your wicked way with him? As a Dominant, you enjoy planning a scenario and being in command of how it unfolds. You're the director, you're in charge, and it probably gives you a bit of a power rush.

As a good Dominant, it's your job to take the fantasies of your partner and bring them to life, to create a scene where they can truly let go and be free to surrender control to you in the moment. Your natural counterpart is, of course, a submissive. You'll find countless Dominant/submissive scenes and ideas in this book, as well as a whole chapter dedicated to it.

The submissive (or 'sub')

Dominance and submission is about a power exchange between two consenting adults, so being a sub does not mean being passive. In fact, submission is very active in that it's an independent choice to serve or be dominated, and you ardently enjoy it.

Perhaps you had fantasies as a child of being the damsel in distress, bound and captured? Maybe you like having your hair pulled, being spanked or pinned down? Perhaps you like the idea of a sexually confident, assertive woman who takes what she wants from you and uses you to satisfy her own desires?

Giving someone power over you sexually can be liberating. With someone you trust and within the boundaries of your pre-defined limits, you give up control and responsibility for what happens. There's also a huge rush in the act of serving someone and being their 'sex slave' for a while.

Naturally, a Dominant is the best match for you if you're sexually submissive. You'll find chapters here on Domination/ submission and Femdom, but since power exchange features prominently in lots of sex play there are elements of it in almost every chapter.

The switch

Some people like to dominate at times and submit at others. If that's you, you're what's called a switch.

In my opinion, switches have the best of both worlds: the full rush of power when they dominate and the blissful release of surrender when they submit. Although you might have a preference for domination or submission, the role you take depends largely on your partner's preferences or the mood you're in. And whilst some switches are very much split between the two, others prefer to dominate or submit perhaps 90% of the time, switching only with partners they deeply trust.

If you're a switch, any sort of relationship with an erotic power exchange component will be fulfilling, but if you're with someone who's 100% Dom(me) or sub there's a chance you could find yourself frustrated. A fellow switch will be the perfect match for you.

Bondage

What better way to give yourself up to the delights of sensual pleasure than being bound? There's something exhilarating about being powerless to do anything but revel in the delights your lover bestows on you. It also feels vulnerable so bondage appeals to many submissives, though by no means all.

Many Dominants love to tie up their partners or in some way restrain them. There are several ways to tie someone up or down and you don't need to know fancy knots, as you'll see in the chapter dedicated to bondage.

Kinky

It sounds like you're eager for sexual exploration and have fantasies you'd like to fulfil. The word 'kinky', for so long maligned, is worn like a badge of honour these days. If you're just dipping your toe in the water, look out for the 'Where do I start?' and 'How do I bring it up?' sections at the beginning of each chapter in Part II. And if you'd like a printable version of this quiz for your lover or a friend, just go to http://bit.ly/K9UwiY and download it.

Up for experimenting but don't quite know how? Then pay special attention to how you react when you read each section of this book. There's a whole world out there for you to explore, so let's get started!

CHAPTER 3
....

HOW TO FIND A SEXUALLY COMPATIBLE LOVER

Dating websites get it all wrong – they'd have much more luck if they matched couples on sexual compatibility instead of interests and eye colour. If you've ever fallen for someone who's not sexually compatible, you know just how much it sucks.

The good news is if you're single, this chapter will give you all the tools you need to find the lover of your dreams. Many people enjoy sexual exploration; you just need the skills to find and recognise them.

This chapter reveals:

- Where to find a compatible lover, in the real world and online
- How to discover someone's secret sexual personality
- How to attract the right lover with hints and signals
- When and how to broach the topic of kinky sex with a potential partner

WHERE DO I START?

If you've done the quiz in the previous chapter you're much closer to knowing and understanding your own turn-ons.

Coming to accept them, however, may be a different matter – and if you don't accept them, how will anyone else?

When I first started exploring my own submissive side I was too embarrassed even to talk to friends about it, so I turned to online kinky communities. Doing research and talking to people online who shared my interests developed my confidence, and it can do the same for you.

Fetlife.com is the best (and largest) international kinky community site for exploring your interests. Think of it as a global knowledge bank for how to be great in bed. You can post questions, read threads on your areas of interest, join groups and talk to people who are coming to terms with their own desires. I used it as a kind of online support group to build my self-acceptance and knowledge. It worked brilliantly. If you want to build self-confidence with the reassurance of anonymity, I thoroughly recommend you do the same.

The more comfortable you are with talking about your desires the more at ease you'll be bringing up the topic with a potential partner. You'll also need a simple, non-threatening way to explain your interests. Use the ideas in this chapter to find what works for you.

Then, practise talking about your sexual preferences with close friends – you might be surprised to hear what they get up to behind closed doors. You never know, saying "Why can't I find a guy who's into ___?" may just have your friends clamouring to introduce you to one of their buddies!

WHERE DO I GO TO MEET KINKY PEOPLE?

Kinky people are everywhere – in the supermarket, the cinema, clubs, bars and yes, even at work. Dating is a numbers game so I'd advise you to simply keep meeting as many single people as you can. You'll get plenty of ideas of how to broach the topic of kinky sex with someone you like later in this chapter.

In addition to places like friends' parties, social events and bars, consider laid-back events with a kinky twist. These could include risqué film festivals, erotic art exhibitions, educational workshops and book launches by sex book authors. Such settings are low-pressure and are likely to attract people with more explorative tastes. Best of all you'll easily be able to start conversations with people about the film or works of art you just saw.

> *Guys, please, please have the guts to bring it up beforehand rather than suddenly launching this stuff on a girl. I can't believe the number of men who've tried to spank me during sex when, in fact, my tastes swing entirely in the opposite direction!* **– Sandra**

DISCOVER SOMEONE'S SECRET SEXUAL PERSONALITY

As we all know, a well-mannered gentleman can be a bad boy in the bedroom and that sweet, shy girl might turn out to be a feisty little minx once she's in the mood. So is there a way to tell if someone's dominant, into bondage or even just sexually adventurous? The answer is yes, sometimes.

Voyeurs are fairly easy to spot. They're the types who like to sit back and watch, sitting on the sidelines to observe people's interactions. You'll often find them checking you out when they think you aren't looking. They'll probably use visual language like "see what I mean?" or "get the big picture" and may draw things to explain them to you. They often have an interest in photography or cinema.

Exhibitionists are harder to recognise. Some of them will dress flamboyantly and enjoy being the centre of attention, but sometimes this is more about their social personality than their sexual one. Just because someone's an extrovert doesn't mean they're an exhibitionist.

Dominants, submissives and switches are some of the hardest to spot because their public personas are often at total odds with their private ones. That said, there are ways to form an educated guess.

It's a huge generalisation, but often someone who is very assertive in their professional life is submissive in the bedroom (and vice versa). The jewellery a woman wears often gives away her tendencies, even if her desires are as yet unexplored. If she likes the idea of bondage or submission she might wear choker necklaces or tight, wrist-hugging bracelets which resemble shackles. I myself have worn this type of jewellery since my teens; I always loved the feeling of constriction but never really connected it to the fantasies of bondage and submission I'd had ever since puberty.

Dominants are often outwardly laid-back, sometimes even quiet, but have an authoritative inner core that they show in private. So if you suspect someone to be dominant, test them out by giving a few direct orders like "pour the wine" or "lay the table". A Dom(me) won't usually just mindlessly comply. Often there'll be a little push-back even if it's just a cheeky comment, sardonic smile or raised eyebrow.

When it comes to dominant women, many don't know they will enjoy dominating until they try it so you might not know before you get sexually involved. Be patient and introduce your ideas slowly. The next chapter will show you how.

If you're looking for a submissive man, the odds are stacked in your favour. They are extremely common so you can use the techniques in the 'When and how to broach kinky sex with a potential partner' section later in this chapter.

ATTRACT THE RIGHT LOVER WITH HINTS AND SIGNALS

While you're busily sleuthing for clues as to your date's sexual persona, make no mistake – they're doing the same with you! Sending out flirty hints about your own proclivities gives you a low-risk way to get them to share theirs.

The key is to subtly weave your topic into the conversation. For instance, if you're a girl who likes your hair being pulled, steer the conversation to your school days and mention a boy in your class who used to pull a girl's hair when he liked her. Shoot your date a cheeky little smile and say, "funny how little some things change!"

Then, most importantly, watch closely for his reactions. Do his pupils dilate? Does he smile knowingly? Does he flirt back? Do his eyes glitter? Does he catch his breath or lean forward with increased interest?

> *I bring my kinky side up early and offer it to him like it's a gift – this is fun stuff he gets to do because he's with me! Lucky him, his new girlfriend's smart, hot, fun and a little kinky! If he's keen, brilliant – if not, I break it off. Not everyone is going to be right for me. But usually the guy gives it a go because he knows it turns me on. I've corrupted a lot of good boys that way.* **– Kirsten**

Use an even more direct approach in a party situation when talking in a group. Just say something like, "Hey, we were just talking about something. What do you think: hair pulling – sexy or not?"

The 'sexy or not?' approach works best if you appear to be asking an impromptu question on the back of a conversation you were just having and deliver your question playfully. So you could ask, "Hey, we were just discussing something. What do you think: spanking – sexy or not?" or "Being tied down – sexy or not?" – or even "Latex catsuits – sexy or not?"

The opportunities are endless. You can even use your question as a way to start a game, with each person in the group asking a 'sexy or not?' question of their own.

Again, don't just listen to what someone says – look closely for body language clues. People are often too shy to confess their desires in public, but if you see them suddenly perk up you're probably on the right track.

WHEN SHOULD I BRING IT UP?

I often speak to people with beautiful, multi-faceted kinky imaginations who are years into their marriages before they discover their partner isn't interested in anything but vanilla sex, and never will be. Tragically, by that time there's nothing they can do about it.

So what can you do to avoid getting stuck in a sexually frustrating relationship with someone you're not compatible with? You'll be doing both of you a favour by broaching the subject of kinky sex early on. And yes, that's true even if your date thinks you're a freak – or if they tried what you're into before and hated it – because in that case you're probably not right for each other, and it's best to discover that sooner rather than later.

As I've said before, sex is the one thing we do in a relationship that we can't do with anyone else, so sexual compatibility is vital to prevent things fizzling out. And the great thing is you don't need every date to go well. You're not recruiting for a harem, just searching for one person who's a good match for you. So keep dating until you find them.

Is your date kink-curious?

Remember, it's common at the start of a relationship to talk about each other's turn-ons, and many of us are curious about potentially pushing our boundaries. It's not essential that your date has tried specific things, but before you invest time and energy in a relationship you'll want to know that he or she is at least open to experimenting.

Discussing sex doesn't mean you have to jump into bed early on, either. Drawing out each other's turn-ons over a succession of dates before doing the deed builds anticipation and arousal, as well as trust. The information you have about each other's likes and dislikes will make your first-time sex electric.

Some people end up trying things like sensation play or bondage because their lover introduces them to it. When they do they often find they like it, especially if they see how turned on it gets their lover. On the other hand, if your date simply isn't interested in talking about such things you're probably incompatible, much as you would be if you didn't share the same values.

HOW TO MEET A KINKY PARTNER ONLINE

Online dating can work well for finding a kinky love – or you can fall flat on your face. In my experience, aside from a few rare exceptions, sites like Collarme.com, Alt.com or AdultMatchMaker.com mainly attract people looking for casual hook-ups, sex workers and married men.

You'll have much better luck with the largest international kink community site in the world, Fetlife.com, which I mentioned earlier. Often dubbed 'The Facebook of Fetish', it's not a dating site but there are lots of groups you can join to talk about your interests and connect with likeminded people. It's respectful, has a community feel and is a great source of information on parties, educational workshops, events and munches in your area. Going along to events like these can be a great way to connect with like-minded kinky people in a no-pressure, social way. And you never know where that might lead.

Munch – A meeting of a group of kinky people, usually in a pub or restaurant, for the purpose of networking, discussion and making new friends. Munches are arranged in each city and the best way to find out about them is on www.Fetlife.com. They are simply a chance to meet and chat with other kinky people rather than pick up, but I know of a few couples who've met at them.

Out of all the online options, however, the best reports I've had are about the free site OkCupid.com which typically attracts a less mainstream crowd than sites like RSVP.com. au, EHarmony.com and Match.com. That's because OKCupid is the site that's the closest to matching you on the basis of sexual compatibility. Just answer all the survey questions and quizzes that will signal to their robots that you're 'more kinky', and you'll attract both curious newbies and more experienced kinky people.

You can also list your main interests in your profile and mention in passing that you're kinky. Keep it playful, perhaps describing your ideal guy as 'a gentleman in the street who's a bad boy in the sheets'. If you're a man, steer well clear of any even vaguely sleazy behaviour. And yes guys, that definitely includes posting cock pictures.

Don't rule out conventional online dating sites either. There are ways to signal your interests, even if they're as simple as listing *The Secretary* in your favourite films.

If you've met someone online, messaging each other about your desires before meeting in person can help establish whether you're likely to be sexually compatible, as you can see in the following story.

First Kiss

As we park outside my house I'm thinking, this man just drips sex appeal. I mean it oozes from every pore. And best of all, though it's been a normal first date, from our chats online I know he's a Dom. A Dom with a creatively filthy imagination.

"Good night," I say reaching for the car door handle, but he doesn't reply. His deep brown eyes are filled with unnervingly raw lust as he holds my gaze.

I'm transfixed. He leans towards me, hand snaking behind my neck to softly cup the back of my head. He runs his fingers up through my hair. So, so slowly.

Our lips meet and suddenly, without warning, it happens. He grabs me firmly by the hair and pulls, and with that single act my whole world falls away.

I'm panting. No first kiss ever felt like this. This is not polite, this is just not done – this is just fantastic. Within a second like a stone I've dropped deep into the ecstasy of subspace. I've heard about this, but never lived it. I am both sinking and flying – I was born to have this feeling!

Still gripping my hair he pulls away. I'm breathless with desire. I want more – more than I've ever wanted anything in my life – but I know it's not my place to ask.

With calm detachment his eyes lazily scan my body as though I'm an interesting specimen for him to toy with. He leans in and his warm breath on my ear makes me shiver.

He pauses for the longest time, then softly whispers, "You want to serve me, don't you? You're desperate to serve me. You crave to serve me. I can tell." I manage to moan a yes through my gasps.

And I'm his, completely his. Dear God I have waited for this feeling my entire life! Everything dissolves. There's no past, no future, nothing and no one except our all-consuming need: his to control me and mine to be controlled.

WHEN AND HOW TO BROACH KINKY SEX WITH A POTENTIAL PARTNER

So you've met people you find attractive, stayed alert for clues and sent out some hints of your own. Things look good but you still don't know for sure... so how do you bite the bullet and ask them directly?

For a long time I struggled with this one. I didn't want to waste months of my time and risk falling in love, only to discover the guy I was dating's idea of kinky was missionary with the lights on. But on the other hand, bringing it up in the first few dates was terrifying!

Then one day, when I was bewailing my situation to my friend Javier, he gave me an answer that changed everything. He has a low-pressure, fun way to discover what someone is into on the very first date – and as I discovered when I tried it myself, it really works!

"Let's play a game," he says to his date. "Hold on, I'm thinking this up as I go along." This of course is a total fib, but it's in a good cause.

"The first rule," he continues, "is that you ask a question and then I ask a question. The second rule is that neither of us can ask a question the other person's already asked. Thirdly, the questions need to be interesting – no boring questions. And the fourth rule is, you go first!"

Typically the girl will say "no, you go first!" which allows him to seem extra-gallant by saying "OK, but if you break that rule it means you have to keep all the others."

His first question is something fairly innocuous like "How old were you when you had your first boyfriend?" But as the questions continue he escalates things, and so does she. Before long he's asking questions like "What's your favourite sexual position?" and it doesn't take long before he gets away with questions like "Have you ever tried bondage?"

If you keep things playful and have fun with it, this technique works a treat. Try it out on your next first date and see for yourself.

Another alternative is just to be direct. If you know what you want, often the best way to get it is to ask for it.

One way is to leap straight in on your first date and ask, "Ever done anything kinky?" Alternatively leave it for a couple of dates and once you're opening up about things have a nice, long conversation about both of your desires, turn-ons and preferences. Starting that kind of conversation shows confidence and builds trust fast, and with the right approach it can be pretty hot.

Bringing up your sexual desires with a potential partner can be nerve-wracking, especially if you've been ridiculed, called a freak or rejected by previous partners. If that's the case, it may help to remind yourself that though not fictional, your own personal experience has its limits. You haven't yet met every possible potential lover – so go out there and start looking!

CHAPTER 4
....

HOW TO GET YOUR LOVER INTO KINKY SEX

I t's impossible to get someone to do something unless they want to do it. But hold on, are you *sure* your partner's not open to kinky sex?

Being a good lover is like being a detective, sleuthing out what really turns your lover on. In this chapter we'll explore how to build a sexually exciting, adventurous relationship by tapping into your creativity so you'll never run out of new ideas.

Specifically, you'll discover how to:

- Bring up fantasies you'd like to explore without risking rejection
- Connect more deeply with your lover
- Discover your lover's fantasies and how to push their hot buttons
- Turn your partner on with dirty talk
- Turn your fantasies into fact

WHAT IF MY LOVER'S ONLY EVER EXPERIENCED VANILLA SEX?

Lack of experience doesn't equate to lack of enthusiasm. There are all sorts of reasons why your lover may have had only vanilla sex. Perhaps they've always fantasised about doing kinky stuff but have been too scared of being called a freak to voice their desires. Maybe a previous lover ridiculed or abandoned them over their sexual interests and they've responded by burying them.

Sometimes, people simply lack the imagination or knowledge to think up new things to try – which doesn't mean they wouldn't try them if they had an experimental lover (like you!) to suggest things. Others may have had a highly repressive upbringing that makes them feel guilty for exploring their sexual persona. (Actually, these pressure-cooker types often make wonderfully kinky lovers if you give them a safe way to let off steam, but you'll need to communicate lots.)

Unfortunately, there are some things that you're not going to get past. A low or non-existent sex drive will obviously create problems if yours is high. There are also those who point-blank rule out any explorative sex whatsoever, and are perfectly fulfilled by vanilla sex only. And no judgements here folks – that's just how some people roll.

BRINGING UP YOUR FANTASIES WITHOUT RISKING REJECTION

Firstly, learn to accept yourself and your desires. As I said in the previous chapter, if *you* don't think your interests are OK, how can you expect your lover to? The more comfortable you begin to feel with yourself, the more confident you'll come across when you discuss what you want. Hey, you may even develop a sense of humour about it!

If you have one particular thing you'd like to try, begin by researching it online and reading about it in this book. How common is it? Are there any safety concerns and if so, what do you need to do to keep you and your partner safe? What is the media saying about it? Times change fast and activities that were 'out' yesterday may be 'in' today just by virtue of the latest music video, paperback or blockbuster movie.

If you're feeling brave, talk to a few close friends and find out if they have any experience with it. As the following personal experience illustrates, you'll often be surprised at what you discover.

Spanking confessions

I had a huge complex about bringing up my penchant for spanking in relationships until I spoke about it to an old school friend who was visiting me from the UK.

As I told her, every guy I'd suggested spank me would look at me in a slightly bewildered way and then respectfully oblige. He'd pop me over his knee and after each thwack, like the gentleman he was, would tentatively ask, "Is this OK? Did that hurt?" Needless to say, he didn't quite get the idea. It's a lonely feeling to be politely spanked.

At the time, I told my friend this was all because these men just weren't natural Dominants. Now I know better. I simply didn't communicate what I wanted them to do, how hard I wanted to be hit, what the fantasy was all about and what they should say while they did it. And most importantly, I failed to reassure these highly considerate men that I would *definitely* speak up if they ever hurt me in a not-so-fun way.

It astounded me to discover my British school friend on the other hand had the exact same interests, but met plenty of guys who loved nothing better than to give her a good over-the-knee spanking! As she said just before she left, "You're so feisty Jess; I think you'll be hard pushed to find a guy who *doesn't* secretly want to put you over his knee. You just need to make it OK for him to do it, and show him exactly how."

CONNECT MORE DEEPLY WITH YOUR LOVER

Now you're more confident about your desires, it's time to open the door to some honest conversations. How? By trading sex secrets.

Couples who don't talk about sex tend to get stuck in a rut, never trying anything new because they assume they're both happy with things the way they are. Talking about sex helps you get into your lover's head and understand what makes him or her tick. Best of all, it warms them up to eventually revealing their secret desires.

Find the idea of having a proper conversation about sex with your lover daunting? It helps if you choose a time away from the bedroom when you're both relaxed. So go out to a restaurant, chat over a glass of wine or go for a walk.

Keep things light, fun and playful and be sure to share things about yourself as well as asking questions. The aim here is simply to build trust, connection and intimacy, so no hanky-panky — yet!

Exchanging sex secrets is another step to opening the door to more explicit conversations about what each of you wants to try. Here are some sex secret questions to help you get to know the roots of your lover's desires.

- How did you first learn about sex? Who told you about it, how old were you and how did you react?
- Who was the first person you had a crush on and how did you know them?
- How old were you when you first kissed, and what was the experience like?
- What was your first sexual experience of any kind?
- How old were you when you first had sex? How did you find it?
- Who did you confide in about sex when you were growing up?
- What were your parents' attitudes to sex? How do you think they influenced you?
- What religion were you raised in? How do you think it influenced what you think of as acceptable and unacceptable sex?
- What was your most embarrassing sexual moment?
- What sexy dreams have you had?
- Do you masturbate? If so, how often and in what way?
- What unexpected thoughts, situations or visual cues turn you on?
- Which parts of your body do you most like to have touched?
- What are some of the most experimental sexual things you've done?

- If you could try just one sexual thing you've never experienced, what would it be?

HARNESS THE POWER OF THE F-WORD

The F-Word is a powerful secret weapon which, used correctly, will unlock the door to experimental sex and help you create the exciting, adventurous relationship you've always dreamed of. 'F' stands for 'Fantasy' – without a doubt the sexiest word in the dictionary.

Sharing your fantasies takes you to a new level of intimacy, building a sexual terrain that belongs uniquely to the two of you. You're connecting with each other in a way you will only ever experience with that one person – and that's what makes this such a passionate, romantic journey.

DISCOVER YOUR LOVER'S FANTASIES AND HOW TO PUSH THEIR HOT BUTTONS

You've talked about sex in society, you've traded sex secrets, now you're ready to discuss your fantasies. Keep things light and playful and set up a safe, no-judgement zone for talking about your desires. Give each other the go-ahead to mention whatever wild, wonderful kinky play you wish. After all, a fantasy is just a fantasy – you don't need to act it out.

There are a few ways to create low-pressure situations that encourage openness and sharing. Remember, it's easier to get your partner to open up if you share one of your fantasies first. Why not start a sexy conversation via text, email or instant messenger? Often it's much easier to reveal your desires in writing than in person. This technique is also perfect for keeping the spark alive in long-distance relationships.

If you're a sexual adventurer with much more experience than your lover, tone it right down. Tell one of your milder fantasies first, then ask about theirs. Embellish their fantasies with things you think would turn them on and create something together that will satisfy you both.

Living together? If you're shy about talking about your desires, make a 'fantasy box'. Whenever the mood takes you, just write a fantasy on a piece of paper and put it in the box. Pull one out every week and talk about it. If you're brave enough, and you both find it hot, you can even act it out.

Once you start talking about your fantasies you'll find that you cross over into the zone of Dirty Talk. This is great news because it's a way to use flirtatious, playful language to unveil your lover's secret sexual interests.

Nervous or shy about talking dirty?

Ironically it can often be a real turn-on when someone looks uncomfortable talking dirty, so don't be too concerned if you're embarrassed. If it's your partner who's shy, that can work in your favour too. Make it a game. Coax them with something they want (a massage, a cooked dinner) if during erotic play they repeat the words that turn you on. Once they see how much it excites you to hear them, they'll probably be eager to say them again.

TURN YOUR LOVER ON WITH DIRTY TALK

Imagine being able to get your partner wet or hard with just a few choice words. Dirty talk can turn a snatched half-hour lunch break into an intensely erotic tease-and-denial experience and keep the spark there no matter how long you've been together.

When you're in an aroused state, words that could otherwise seem degrading are often quite hot. The important thing is that you're both getting off on what you're saying to each other. It's OK to go there in the heat of the moment: you can have the deepest respect for your partner and still call her a 'whore' in bed if that's what turns her on. Dirty talk doesn't define the dynamics of your relationship; you're not actually pledging to be their sex slave!

> *I had issues talking dirty when I was younger as I just wasn't very confident. My wife was the one who initiated me, and now I realise how it heightens the intensity between us so I do it all the time. Nothing gets me harder than hearing the rise of her moans when I call her names.* **– Simon**

Drawing out dirty talk over hours or even days builds sexual tension, which is what makes us crave sex. The slow, tantalising build-up helps keep it exciting, and receiving a sexy text is sure to make that dull meeting you're in a lot more interesting.

Best of all, used in the bedroom, a few carefully chosen words can be just the thing to tip your lover over into that earth-shattering orgasm they've been teetering on the edge of.

Dirty and delicious

I hold my hands up – I used to find dirty talk cringingly embarrassing. I was raised to be a good British girl, never to swear and not to mention sex in polite company. My parents did the right thing and told me the facts of life but they forgot to mention one important detail: sex feels good!

As a consequence, I'm delighted to report that my mind became a frisky little pressure-cooker of raunchy ideas and filthy bad-girl words. You can imagine what happened when I met the lucky lad who lifted the lid.

Now a veteran in dirty talk, I relish its naughtiness and get a playful little thrill from throwing the odd word out in polite company in my posh British accent to test someone's reactions. I know it's possible to give my lover an instant hard-on wherever we are, just by holding his gaze and saying a few choice words in a low, sexy voice. Trust me, the power rush is incredible!

Talking dirty is easy: it's just about discovering your lover's trigger words and using them when you speak. But to seek out those precious little words that drive your lover wild, you'll need to ask questions and *listen carefully.*

Pick a time when you're both relaxed and away from the bedroom, and ask your lover to describe a fantasy. You can tell them one of your own first if you think it will lower their inhibitions. Make it clear that you won't judge them and you don't necessarily want to act it out, you just think it would be hot to hear. As they begin, encourage them to keep talking by saying how much they're turning you on.

Ask what arouses them about their scenario. When they reply, listen closely to the words they use. These will often be their trigger words. For example, they might say they feel 'naughty' and need to be 'punished'.

Look them in the eye and in a low, confident voice, say a suspected trigger word back to your lover to test its power. As they're telling their story, throw in a flirty little "Oh, you're so naughty," or say, 'I would love to punish you like that.' Watch and listen closely to see how they react. Do they sigh, moan, flush, gasp, lean forward? Do their eyes fill with desire? If they seem to be getting aroused, you've hit on a trigger word. Store it away in your memory like the little gold nugget it is.

Test for related concepts, not just words. For example, you could develop an idea by saying "Naughty girls like you need to be punished. How would you feel if I put you over my knee, lifted your skirt, pulled your panties down and gave you a spanking?" What you're doing here is painting a picture. Again, watch carefully for their reaction. You'll know if you've hit the jackpot.

Once you find a trigger word, test for similar ones. For example, if they like 'punish' you might try 'deserve', 'obedient' or 'discipline', again checking for reactions.

Watch out for words that are turn-offs, too. Just because someone enjoys being called a 'slut' or a 'whore' once in a while during sex play doesn't mean they like being called a 'bitch'. Always pay attention to their non-verbal responses.

Boys like dirty talk, too. Some men enjoy hearing they're being used for your enjoyment. If he's on the dominant side, he might like you to call him Master or Sir, or even to repeat sentences with his trigger words, like 'I'm your fuck-toy, Sir.'

If you're too shy to talk dirty, try playfully reading your lover an erotic story. Again, watch for trigger words and concepts. Skype, phone calls, messaging or even texts are brilliant for discovering each other's trigger words, as you don't have the embarrassment of looking them in the eye when you confess. Here's an example of a conversation that I imagine would be easier to have over the phone than in person. How many trigger words and phrases can you find?

Dirty Dialogue

"I had this fantasy," I say into the phone. "You might think it's a bit freaky."

"Mmmmm...I love it," he says softly. "Every time you say something might freak me out it ends up being a massive turn-on."

"Well this might not," I insist.

"Just tell me," he says, dying to know. I laugh. He's a man after my own heart.

"OK. I imagined you told me I'd been a very bad girl and I needed to be punished. You said you knew what was best for me, and asked me if I would like to receive my punishment."

"Mmmmm." he purrs.

"I said I know Master owns me and Master always knows best, and I would gratefully receive any punishment Master wants to give me."

He moans. I know he gets hard when I call him Master.

"Then you tied my arms and legs down to the bed so I was on my back, legs spread, like you did that other time."

"With the ropes under your knees, anchored to the top bedposts?"

"Exactly! So if I tried to close my knees, I wouldn't be able to."

"Oh this is sounding gooood. Then what?"

"Then you got your riding crop out and stood there over me, slapping it into your hand, saying your slut needs to be punished. You said, would you like Master to punish you?"

"Mmmm."

"And I said yes Master, I know I've been a bad girl. I know Master needs to discipline his slut and I will be so grateful to receive his punishment."

"You would be grateful," he laughs lightly.

"Yes I would!" I giggle back. He really gets me. I love it when we plan scenes like this.

"So you took the riding crop and you positioned it precisely above my pussy, and you gave me a tap with it. I flinched, but it wasn't hard."

"Oh you are such a dirty girl."

"And then you started lightly cropping my pussy lips. Oh my God, it felt so good! Every time I looked up, your eyes would be focused on my pussy, to be sure you cropped me with scientific precision."

"Ohhhh."

"Then you got harder. And every time you hit me I would feel a shot of pain, then a wave of incredible pleasure, and such wonderful humiliation."

"Mmmm, you'd be so helpless. This is incredible."

"Really? You don't think I'm a freak?"

"No! Are you *kidding*?"

"Why do you like it?"

"Mmmm, I would feel so powerful. Tell me the rest."

"And then you told me Master was going to punish my pussy till it was nice and sore for you. So you cropped it, then you spanked it, till I couldn't take any more. I was so sore."

"Wow."

"And then...."

"Yes?"

"This is a little bad..."

"Tell me!"

"OK. You told me you were going to fuck my sore, punished pussy, whether I liked it or not, until you came."

"Oh my God!"

"You grabbed me by the hair and as you pushed your cock inside me I cried out in pain, but you knew I was loving it. You told me to take it for Master, and you looked me in the eye as you fucked me hard. Every time you thrust into me, you would feel pleasure – but I would feel pain."

"Wow!"

"And you fucked me, punishing me with every thrust, till you came – violently, loudly, looking me in the eye the entire time."

Silence.

"Do you think I'm a freak?"

"God no!"

"Then how would it make you feel?"

"Powerful. Really, really powerful. You giving yourself to me like that. Wow that is so hot!"

I laugh, relieved. "We are *such* freaks."

"I know, it's great!" I can hear he's grinning. "So when do we do it?"

I smile. "What are you doing on Friday?"

TURN YOUR FANTASIES INTO FACT

If you have fantasies you'd like to suggest trying, it can be less threatening for your lover if you focus on living out one or more of theirs before turning to your own. Remember, it takes time to explore what turns you both on and create something together.

Going too fast may scare off your lover. So go slow – asking your partner to nibble your nipples may be less confronting than asking to be tied up. There's a lot to be said for introducing your less wild fantasies first.

It's always better to end a scene feeling you could have gone further rather than thinking you've pushed things too far. For example, if you want to try being dominated, skip the elaborate role-play and ask your lover to pin you down and pull your hair. If you're thinking of trying a little bondage, suggest tying your partner up and pleasuring them. And if you want to try pain play, begin with some light nibbling or scratching, increasing the intensity if your partner seems to enjoy it.

Keep it light and flirtatious

Asking your lover to try new things is easier than you think. Try these start lines to get things going.

"You looked so hot in that (dress/suit) yesterday – I haven't been able to stop thinking about you all day. I have this fantasy that you meet me at lunchtime and we..."

"You really bring out the naughty side in me. I'd just love to (insert play activity) to you."

"You know, lately I've been imagining you tying me up and teasing me till I beg you to let me come. Do you think you'd enjoy that?"

"I was reading this book the other day where this couple (insert play activity). Is that something you'd fancy?

"I've been thinking how much fun it would be to try a little (bondage/spanking/role play). Is that something you'd be up for?"

"I'd love to see you (tied up / cooking dinner for me in only an apron / in your hot suit while I'm naked). Would that turn you on?"

"You know, after the other night I think it's time for a little payback. When you get home, I'd like to slowly strip you naked, tie you to the kitchen table and..."

"My imagination's been racing since you told me about that fantasy of yours the other day. How about we try acting it out on Saturday afternoon?"

DO YOUR RESEARCH

Do everything you can to make the encounter as positive as possible and your lover might just want to do it again – and may even want to explore further. So whatever you try, make sure you *read up thoroughly* on it in this book so you can deliver your lover the very safest, most pleasurable experience. If there are specific activities you want to try, look them up in the appropriate chapter and check out the 'Where do I start?' section. I've included lots of tips for broaching each subject in a low-pressure way.

CHAPTER 5
....

HOW TO HEIGHTEN SEXUAL CHEMISTRY

Desire fizzles out when we compartmentalise the erotic aspect of our relationship. We get bored. If we don't flirt, compliment and tease each other during the day, we can't just flick a switch and turn our lover on at night.

But by building desire for each other simultaneously, you'll keep the passion simmering. This chapter shows you how to use kinky sex to ignite that spark between you and keep things exciting. You'll discover how to:

- Set the scene for seduction
- Become irresistible to your lover
- Affair-proof your relationship
- Tap into your sexual creativity so you'll never run out of new ideas
- Use the one technique that makes sex hotter every time

WHERE DO I START?

As mistress of seduction Marlene Dietrich famously said, "The longer they wait, the better they like it". So to increase the sexual intensity between you, synchronise your arousal states with a slow build-up.

Tease each other with texts throughout the day. Tell your lover what you're going to do to them when they get home, what you want them to be wearing, or what position you want them to take as they wait for you. The thrill of anticipation makes the charge electric when you finally touch. That's because anticipation and longing are powerful aphrodisiacs, both essential to sustaining long-term desire. We want what we can't have, so having sex on tap often backfires.

Instead, draw out the time between scenes by flirting, teasing your lover with ideas of what you're going to do to them, and playfully describing the things you want to do the next time you have sex. It's essential to keep some erotic tension if you want things to stay interesting.

Waiting

I wait on all fours for my Master to arrive. The smooth wooden floor feels cold and hard against my hands and knees but I hold the pose perfectly for him, longing to make him proud of me. Blissfully humiliated, I'm shaking with desire and anticipation.

His texts over the past hour specified precisely how to prepare myself for his arrival. As a sign of my submission to him I am to wait in this position, eyes cast down, without speaking, wearing nothing but stockings and high heels. At this time I am purely his sex object.

As the key turns in the door I'm suddenly flustered. My good manners kick in. You're meant to greet someone when they walk into your home, not be waiting on all fours without speaking. I don't know the proper way to behave in this situation and it's thrillingly uncomfortable.

Nervously, I look up to catch his eye. "Eyes down!" he orders. I immediately drop my gaze.

He walks towards me. I have no idea what he will do next and I'm not allowed to look. The anticipation is overwhelming. He circles me languidly, coolly surveying his property. My mind races with all the things he might do to me.

I deeply crave his touch, shaking so hard now. Though I can't see him, I sense he relishes the effect he's having on me. He is tantalisingly close, teasing me with his presence, but he takes his time. The straps of my high heels dig into my ankles. He knows this pose is painful in heels and he understands I hold it as a sign of respect and adoration for him.

After what feels an eternity, he runs a finger slowly down my spine. I am dripping wet and desperate for him.

SET THE SCENE FOR SEDUCTION

In my opinion, spontaneity is over-rated. Planning a scene together, on the other hand, can be part of the sexy lead-up that gives each time you play a real sense of occasion.

If you have kids, it's even more important to make the times when you do have sex feel really special. It can be hard to make time for each other when you've just had a child but even if you're rarely having sex, by building sexual tension you can keep the desire burning.

Planning a scene also gives you the opportunity to stimulate all the senses.

Sight: Make sure the room looks tidy and inviting. Dim any bright lights or light the room with candles and lamps. If you are planning a role play, buy the outfits you're planning to wear; if not, just wear something you know your lover will find sexy.

Touch: Check the temperature of the room is warm enough or cool enough for you and your lover to relax without your clothes on. Have the toys you'll need to hand or pack a toy bag to take to your lover's place. Talking to your lover about what to bring can be part of the tantalising lead-up. Also think about any household items you'd like to use. If, for example, you're planning some temperature play, make sure the ice tray in the freezer is filled up.

Sound: Think carefully about whether you want silence, and if music will add to or detract from the scene. If you both want music, what type will be in keeping with the mood without distracting you?

Scent: Incense, scented candles or essential oils will set the scene. Some of the sexiest scents include jasmine, ylang ylang, patchouli, rose and cinnamon, but scent is a matter of personal taste so it could be best to shop for it together. Think about yourself, too – does your lover like a particular scent you wear, or do they love your natural aroma?

Taste: Whether your lover likes chilled champagne, chocolate or beer, stock the fridge with treats. Food can be a powerful aphrodisiac and a fun, sensual addition to your scene.

Rushing a scene completely kills it, so make sure you both have enough time to fully focus on each other for an agreed amount of time. And switch your phones off!

HOW TO BECOME IRRESISTIBLE TO YOUR LOVER

Here are some more ways to heighten your lover's desire for you. These, when used in tandem with the other concepts in this book, will go a long way to protecting your relationship from the threat of infidelity.

Harness the power of eye contact

A famous experiment by Harvard psychologist Zick Rubin demonstrates just how powerful eye contact is. He created a 'love scale' on which couples who'd been together for several years rated how intense, loving and exciting their relationship was.

When he set cameras up to monitor each couple's eye contact he found a pattern: couples who were deeply in love usually held eye contact 75% of the time while talking (in normal conversation we look at each other only 30 to 60% of the time). It seems extended eye contact makes you more desirable to your lover. But why?

When we lock eyes with someone we find attractive, it's thought we release the feel-good chemical oxytocin, known as the cuddle hormone, as well as the 'falling in love' chemical, PEA. And, of course, eye contact is the best way of staying in tune with your lover during a scene so you can know if they're enjoying something or not.

Keep it exciting

If you run out of ideas, try a new twist on an old favourite. Like it when he gives you oral sex? Then try blindfolding him while he does it this time. If you enjoy the missionary position, try it with one of you tied to the bed. There are endless ways to combine ideas and keep things hot and interesting.

Give great feedback

While you're playing, be sure to show your lover just how much you're enjoying it with plenty of encouraging body language, words and sounds.

Most importantly, be sure to tell them how fantastic it was for you afterwards. They may have been nervous to try something new so getting this reassurance will build their confidence and make them keen to try more next time.

Don't push it

If there's something your lover just isn't into, the worst thing you can do is pressure them. Yes, introducing things slowly and working your way up can work but if, for example, they just really aren't into dominating you, criticising them or making them feel guilty won't change that.

Tap into your creativity for new ideas

The first time I indulged in the delights of kinky sex was with a man I'd been friends with for years who lived a long way away. Because of the trust we'd built through our friendship I was quickly willing to experiment.

We didn't have much time together when I visited so he would instruct me exactly how to prepare for each trip, knowing very well what little sexual experience I'd had. "Write a list," he would say, "of all the things you've always wanted to do but never dared to ask for." Those words were like music to my ears!

Many people find the idea of writing a list of all the kinky things they've ever wanted to do pretty scary. Ticking things off from a pre-written list, however, is quite another matter. So to help you along, here's my Lover's List of ideas to get you started.

Go through and circle 'green' for things you want to try, 'amber' for things you'd only try under certain conditions, and 'red' for total no-goes. Make sure you say whether you'd like to give or receive, and feel free to add any ideas of your own in the space provided at the end. If you don't know what something is, don't worry; you'll get full explanations in Part II of this book.

Once you've made your selections, put a strip of paper over your column and give the list to your lover, without revealing your answers. I guarantee the results will give you plenty to explore! To download this list for free, go to http://thekinkysexbook.com/lovers-list/.

THE LOVERS' LIST

	You	Your Lover
Blindfolding	Green Amber Red	Green Amber Red
Temperature play	Green Amber Red	Green Amber Red
Sensory deprivation	Green Amber Red	Green Amber Red
Sex toys	Green Amber Red	Green Amber Red
Tickling	Green Amber Red	Green Amber Red

Biting	Green	Amber	Red	Green	Amber	Red
Hair pulling	Green	Amber	Red	Green	Amber	Red
Pinching	Green	Amber	Red	Green	Amber	Red
Spanking	Green	Amber	Red	Green	Amber	Red
Paddling	Green	Amber	Red	Green	Amber	Red
Orgasm control	Green	Amber	Red	Green	Amber	Red
Bondage	Green	Amber	Red	Green	Amber	Red
Sex outdoors	Green	Amber	Red	Green	Amber	Red
Electrical play	Green	Amber	Red	Green	Amber	Red
Tie and tease	Green	Amber	Red	Green	Amber	Red
Anal sex	Green	Amber	Red	Green	Amber	Red
Anal stimulation	Green	Amber	Red	Green	Amber	Red
Hot wax play	Green	Amber	Red	Green	Amber	Red
Videoing	Green	Amber	Red	Green	Amber	Red
Role play	Green	Amber	Red	Green	Amber	Red
Costumes	Green	Amber	Red	Green	Amber	Red
Latex	Green	Amber	Red	Green	Amber	Red
Lingerie	Green	Amber	Red	Green	Amber	Red
Nipple clamps	Green	Amber	Red	Green	Amber	Red
Foot worship	Green	Amber	Red	Green	Amber	Red

Domination/submission	Green Amber Red	Green Amber Red
Collar and leash training	Green Amber Red	Green Amber Red
Eye contact restriction	Green Amber Red	Green Amber Red
Speech restriction	Green Amber Red	Green Amber Red
_____	Green Amber Red	Green Amber Red
_____	Green Amber Red	Green Amber Red
_____	Green Amber Red	Green Amber Red
_____	Green Amber Red	Green Amber Red
_____	Green Amber Red	Green Amber Red
_____	Green Amber Red	Green Amber Red

THE ONE TECHNIQUE THAT MAKES SEX HOTTER EVERY TIME

If you've followed the steps above for dirty talk, you'll already be exploring your lover's turn-ons and fantasies. Taking these to the next level – planning to act them out – is one part of what's called **negotiation**.

Negotiation, done well, builds your knowledge of each other's turn-ons so that rather than becoming dull, sex just gets hotter and hornier every time. It's an incredibly effective, simple technique. Here's how it works.

1. Before play

- Decide which of you or your lover's fantasies you'd both like to try. As in the phone conversation above, if you lead on from 'talking dirty' this should be pretty easy. The Lover's List exercise might also be a good place to start.

- Define what hard and soft limits each of you have (see the boxed text below).

- Plan which toys or outfits you will need for the scene, if any.

- Establish a safeword. This is a word which, if said by either of you, immediately calls a halt to the scene. Sometimes saying 'stop! No!' may be part of a role play, so it's better to choose something more obscure than this for a safeword.

You may never have to use your safeword, but it's good to have one just in case. For example you can use 'red' to say 'slow down, that's getting a bit much' and 'red, red, red' to say 'stop'. If it won't be possible to speak (for example, if you're gagged) you'll need to agree on a non-verbal signal too, like a head shake or hand movement.

Hard limit: This is something that must not be done under any circumstances. What may be a hard limit for one person could be fair game to another – for example one hard limit for me is wax play, but for many this is considered very tame. Because we all have different hard limits, it's important for you and your lover to clearly define what yours are.

Hard limits can change with time: with more experience you might like to try something that was previously a total no-go. If that happens, talk to your partner about it.

Soft limit: A soft limit is something you don't usually want to do except under certain conditions. For example there are many deeply intimate acts that I won't perform unless I'm in a correspondingly intimate, committed relationship. Sometimes a soft limit can be something you like the idea of but need your lover to be cautious about exploring, so defining where you draw those lines before you play is essential.

2. During play

If you're dominating, stay alert to your lover's responses and occasionally check in with them.

- Closely observe their body language, facial expressions and the sounds they make to see what they're most enjoying so you can give them more of it. Giveaway signs they're enjoying things are faster breathing, gasps, moans, increased muscle tension and perhaps even a 'sex flush' across their chest.

- If you're trying something new, directly ask for feedback. A simple 'good?' or 'how are you doing?' whispered in their ear every so often will confirm you're on the right track and show you care.

3. After play

Your lover might feel vulnerable or embarrassed about trying something new, and if so they'll need reassurance. Take time to cuddle, chat and connect afterwards. This is part of what's known as 'Aftercare', and it's an extremely important bonding time when the dominant partner cares for the submissive and you both wind down and come back to reality. Many consider it one of the most loving, rewarding experiences you can share with each other.

SAFETY FIRST!

Aftercare is a key part of keeping your submissive emotionally safe, since it can prevent negative emotional aftereffects such as guilt or what's called 'subdrop', a kind of mood slump that can occur for some people.

Some scenes can be physically and psychologically intense, especially if you're pushing each other's boundaries. Often the submissive's body temperature drops, causing them to shiver, even if they're clothed, so you'll need a warm robe or blanket to hand. If they're still feeling blissed out from the experience, they may be unsteady on their feet and need somewhere comfortable to lie down.

Care given by the Dom(me) may also include cuddling, giving the submissive something to drink or eat, affectionate touching, reassurance or keeping them away from bright light and noise. For many, aftercare is the most rewarding moment of the entire scene, so leave plenty of time for both of you to hold each other and wind down.

After the scene has ended it's a good idea to talk to your lover about how you both felt, what you enjoyed and what you'd like to explore more of another time. You can either do this while you're cuddled up during aftercare or leave it till a few hours later.

Talk about how you both found the experience. For many, the best time to do this is around half an hour after play when you're both floating hazily in post-coital bliss and indulging in pillow talk. I'd also recommend checking in with each other the next day when you've both had a chance to process things. This can be as simple as asking questions like "How did you feel about the way we had sex last night? What did you enjoy most about it? What would you like us to do differently next time? What else would you like to explore?"

Trying new things means there'll be times when you or your partner respond in a way you didn't anticipate, perhaps even with a negative reaction. If you find something didn't go as expected or if you just didn't enjoy it, that's OK – you're exploring, and by its very nature exploration means you don't always find what you're looking for.

What's important is to learn from your experiences and share what you discover so you both gain knowledge about what works for you and what doesn't. Whether you liked something you tried or not, you've just gained new insight into how to please yourself and your partner – which means when you play next time, it'll be even better.

PART II
GETTING IT ON

Now you've charged your erotic imagination, it's time to take the plunge – and this section shows you how. You'll find lots of ideas here to try with your lover, some of which will appeal more than others. Embrace your sense of adventure but don't feel you have to do everything. Start slow, go at your own pace, and approach things with an open mind. Above all, have fun with it!

Warning – you are entering a sex toy wonderland!

Kinky fun can great fun with just your imagination, but I'd be lying to you if I said sex toys aren't fun.

You're about to enter the main part of the book, where I mention some of the highest quality, most pleasure-enhancing sex toys in the world. But many of you have asked me 'Where do I buy them from at the best prices?'

So I've compiled my free 'Secret Sex Toy Guide', which lists every single sex toys I talk about here, by chapter. You'll find everything that could possibly tickle your fancy at awesome prices, sold by reliable suppliers who'll send them to you in discreet packaging.

To access my free 'Secret Sex Toy Guide', just go to http://thekinkysexbook.com/secret-sex-toys/.

CHAPTER 6
....

SENSATION PLAY

O f all the places to begin your explorations, sensation play is the least intimidating. It's all about discovering the sensual ecstasies your bodies are capable of – and who doesn't want to do that?

Sensation play is the perfect way to get to know your lover's physical turn-ons and erogenous zones, and to give and receive fantastic sensations that aren't only genitally focused. Your lover's skin is the largest organ of their body and you'll be learning to play it like a musical instrument. It'll take time to develop an ear for what works but with the ideas in this chapter, you'll have great fun finding out! You'll discover:

- Four steps to sensational stimulation
- Top mild sensations to try
- How to add sexy surprises with contrasting sensations
- Safe, sensual ways to play with hot wax
- How to make sex electric – literally!

If you have a sensual approach to sexual exploration, you'll love sensation play because it relies on surprises and erotic stimuli rather than psychological power exchange. It can also be the answer to the question "So I've tied my lover up – what's next?"

Blocking out your lover's sight, and possibly their hearing, allows them to focus more acutely on the feelings you're giving them, so it's a perfect place to start if you're initially embarrassed about role playing or talking dirty.

At its simplest, sensation play involves creating unusual sensations in your lover: hot, cold, rough, smooth, nibbling, scratching, stroking; the list goes on. In fact most people have experimented with sensation play at some point without knowing it, perhaps running a feather over your lover's body or dragging ice cubes across their skin.

> *For me, sensation play is about communicating without having to be verbal. It's the best way I've found to get to know my girlfriend's body, right down to how a single, light touch in the right place can throw her into ecstasy. There's always something new to discover.* **– Sebastian**

HOW DO I BRING UP SENSATION PLAY WITH MY LOVER?

This one's actually pretty easy to approach. Just tell them it's their lucky night – that you have all sorts of wonderful feelings you're going to give them, and all they have to do is lie back and enjoy!

Begin with milder sensations and work up to more intense ones. As always, stay in tune with your lover and occasionally ask for feedback.

WHERE DO I START?

Like most kinky play, sensation play benefits from a certain amount of planning. You'll need the objects you're going to use close to hand, so think through what you're going to do and get things ready. Fill that ice tray, buy those strawberries, give the jelly time to set and keep all the fun toys you'll need close to hand!

Start simply with a blindfold: taking away the sensation of sight magnifies every touch. Since you can't see anything you won't anticipate what's coming next, which can be incredibly exciting as well as building trust. Not being able to hear amplifies sensations even more.

Sensation play doesn't need to involve blindfolding – you could just close your eyes – but a blindfold really helps you let go and immerse yourself in the experience rather than being tempted to control things by sneaking a peak. You don't need to be tied up either, but ironically there's something freeing about being bound: you can't just remove that blindfold or start pleasuring your lover in return. All you can do is relinquish yourself to the wonderful sensations rushing through you.

The golden rule with sensation play is to always try each thing on yourself before you try it on your lover. You might not think a little candle wax will hurt, but until you try it on yourself you just won't know.

FOUR STEPS TO SENSATIONAL STIMULATION

To give your partner the ultimate sensory experience, enhance their tactile senses by taking their other senses away step by step.

Talk to your lover, using their trigger words as you tie them up (see Chapter 9: Bondage for Beginners for advice on knots to use). Tying your partner makes them completely vulnerable to your touch and enables you to control exactly what they feel.

Blindfold them – an airplane mask works well for this. Go slowly, giving you both time to savour the anticipation of what's to come. Whisper into their ear, tell them how sexy they look all tied up and vulnerable, or that you can't wait for them to discover what you have in store for them.

Check in with them at this point, perhaps with a whispered, 'How're you doing?' If it's their first time, stop here and move on to giving them sensations. If you've done this a few times, you could push your lover's boundaries a little by blocking out their hearing.

You can do this with ear plugs (the soft wax type works best) but these can be fiddly. Noise reduction ear muffs aren't glamorous but they're much more effective! Being unable to hear takes you into another zone where you feel like you're floating, and combined with lack of sight it makes you feel everything much more intensely.

Experiment with different sensations, paying close attention to how your lover moves, breathes and reacts so you can heighten their pleasure with every touch. Even just trailing your fingertips over their body can be extremely erotic. Savour the way their body reacts and play with the sense of surprise: your partner has no idea where you'll touch them next.

TOP MILD SENSATIONS TO TRY

Even the gentlest sensations feel incredibly erotic when your other senses are blocked out. Either use these as a warm-up to more intense play or as an end in themselves – either way, they feel great!

- Feather dusters make great toys and can be used almost anywhere. Try one on your lover's eyelids, nipples, inner thighs, the undersides of their arms, the soles of their feet and their elbow creases.

- If they can hear you, heighten the anticipation by describing in detail what you'll be doing later to each bit of their body as you brush a feather lightly over that part.

- Gently nibble, lick or blow on different areas, closely watching your partner's reactions to see which places they like best.

- Slide your hand up the nape of your lover's neck, grab a fistful of hair and gently grip.

- Drag a cold metal spoon slowly over your lover's skin, up the inside of their thighs or across their perineum. Intensify the feeling by putting the spoon in the freezer for half an hour before you play.

- Run your nails lightly over your lover's ticklish bits. Check beforehand with this one though – some people like being tickled whilst others hate it.

- Ladies: try wearing different types of gloves. Stroking his cock softly or hard while you wear satin gloves can feel wonderful, and some men love the feel of latex or leather gloves.

- Trail silk across your lover's skin. It can feel incredible across his testicles or over her pussy lips.

- Use a vibrator on various parts of the body (this works for both men and women). I recommend the Hitachi Magic Wand: it's the Rolls-Royce of vibrators, delivering a powerful but controllable vibration that's perfect for forcing your lover to orgasm whenever you choose.

- For a unique sensation, use a pen to write or draw over your lover's body. Waiting till after the scene to discover what's written draws out the sense of anticipation for your lover.

The vampire glove

Take it from me – if you haven't experienced the exquisiteness of a vampire glove being dragged slowly and exquisitely across your skin, you haven't lived!

A vampire glove is a soft leather glove with tiny metal spikes protruding from the palm, used to gently stroke the most sensitive parts of the body. Best of all, it's easy to make.

Begin with a pair of soft leather gloves and around twenty thumbtacks (drawing pins). Poke them through from the inside of the palm of the glove in rows and keep going until you've covered the palm in them. Then slip a piece of gaffa tape inside the glove so it lies flush over the thumbtacks, holding them in place.

And there you have it – one delightfully decadent vampire glove, all yours to play with! Drag it gently across your lover's skin for a goose-bump inducing experience. It feels especially good trailed across the inner thighs, elbow creases and the neck.

ADD SEXY SURPRISES BY CONTRASTING SENSATIONS

Mix things up by combining mild sensations with their opposites. Fake fur feels particularly great alternated with cold metal, perhaps with an item from your kitchen utensil drawer. Drag a bamboo skewer lightly across the skin; depending on the pressure it can feel either ticklish or sharp.

The smoothness of silk contrasts wonderfully with the roughness of sandpaper. Or you could begin with the lightest touch of a feather and swap it with the unexpected smack of a ruler. The combinations are endless – you'll get plenty of ideas by just looking around your house.

TEMPERATURE PLAY

Easy and inexpensive, temperature play is a fun addition to your repertoire. Try warming your mouth with some hot tea before sucking on your lover's nipple or trailing your tongue over their body, then taking an ice cube in your mouth and doing the same. This also works well for kissing your blindfolded lover – and feels incredible with oral sex!

WAX PLAY

The ultimate in temperature play is, of course, wax play. Having hot wax drizzled onto your skin can feel very erotic. If you're blindfolded the sense of anticipation is powerful – where will the next drop land? How hot will it be? Sudden heat on the skin can either feel like a shocking surprise or a wonderful release of tension.

Bear in mind, however, that wax play isn't for everyone. Some people love it whilst others only find it painful. I strongly advise trying the wax on yourself, and then on your partner, *before* you begin the scene.

Also remember you're literally playing with fire, and as the person giving the sensations you are responsible for the safety, welfare and pleasure of your partner. Here's how to play with wax safely and sensually.

SAFETY FIRST!

- Check around for anything flammable so you can keep it out of the way. That includes lingerie and your lover's hair. Hairspray is particularly flammable.

- Never leave your partner tied up alone in a room, especially not with a candle burning nearby.

- Have a fire extinguisher and a damp towel to hand just in case.

- To prevent candles being tipped over, bring a hard, flat surface to your play area and place your candles on it.

- Each wax drop causes a certain amount of splatter. Think carefully about your aim, avoiding the eyes, face and any open cuts.

- Never pile hot wax on top of hot wax as it will maintain the heat underneath, which can cause burns.

- Remember, **hot wax burns!** Be careful which type of candles you use, since some of them burn at temperatures that can damage the skin.

Never use:

- Non-drip candles: these contain plasticisers, which make them burn at much hotter temperatures than normal ones.

- Beeswax candles, since they have a naturally high melting point.

- Metallic candles, as they have metal shards in them that will burn into the skin and could scar.

- Anything with additives, as again these can often raise the wax's melting point.

Do use:

- Funnily enough the best candles are often plain old cheap, white paraffin wax candles, the kind you buy in a dollar shop or supermarket. These don't have additives so they burn at low temperatures.

- Soy wax candles, which have an even lower melting point.

- Massage candles such as those from skinnydipcandle. com, which have the lowest melting point of all at just a little over body temperature. Because they contain lotions you can even massage the wax into the skin, adding another layer of sensuality to the experience.

Not sure what sort of wax candle you have?

Test it by cutting a piece of the candle off and rolling it in your hands for a little. If it becomes soft and malleable it's probably made from low-temperature wax like paraffin or soy.

BEFORE YOU BEGIN

Protect your carpet and furniture from wax spills by spreading a tarp, old bed linen or plastic sheet over the area. Gather everything you need: candles, wet cloths, a bowl of ice and any toys you want to use.

Prepare your partner's skin. Wax caught in body hair can be painful and difficult to remove, so if you're using something other than a massage candle you might want to shave any particularly hairy areas. Rub baby oil all over your lover's skin since this makes it easier to remove the wax later. If you're not shaving them, be generous with the oil in areas with body hair.

Always test the candle on yourself before you begin to play by dripping a little wax on the inside of your wrist or forearm. Finally, light a few candles so when you pour the wax from one there will be others ready.

HOW TO DROP THE WAX

Hold the candle around a metre above your lover's body. The higher you are, the cooler the wax will be when it reaches skin. Let the wax pool before dripping it; don't drip wax directly from the flame. Once it's pooled, tilt the candle and allow the molten wax to splash onto your lover's skin.

Drip wax on different areas to create varied sensations. Dripping it on someone's back can feel relaxing, but on the front quite intense. Get to know your partner's body and how it responds. Some favourite areas to try are the back, around the nipples, the buttocks and the backs of the knees. Always stay below the shoulders as the neck and face can burn easily. Avoid the most sensitive areas: the inner thighs, stomach, hips and the genitals.

Watch your lover, not the candle! If they appear to be enjoying things you can intensify the sensation by gradually decreasing the height or increasing the amount of wax you pour. Closely monitor your partner's body and ask for feedback throughout – remember, you're responsible for keeping them safe and giving them a wonderful, erotic experience they'll want to try again. Also be aware that your lover's responses may vary each time you play depending on the warmth of his or her skin, the room temperature – and even, for women, the time of the month.

Peel some of the wax away and alternate the feeling of heat with cool ice or soft fake fur. Try dripping patterns or writing your name. Having wax painted onto your body with a big brush can feel fantastic.

Taking the wax off can be just as much fun as putting it on. Scrape it off with your fingernails or a blunt butter knife, blowing on the skin as you go. Keep things slow and sensual so you can both luxuriate in the experience.

Remove as much wax as possible before your lover showers, as wax tends to block drains. Finally, wash the remaining bits of wax off in the shower with a loofa.

'GUESS THE SENSATION'

This is a fun, light-hearted game that begins with tying your lover to a chair, then blindfolding them. Bring out your toy bag and give them a sensation of your choosing, then stop and order them to guess what it was. If they get it wrong you can invent a consequence or punishment. Perhaps they can perform a sexual favour for you after they're untied, give you a shoulder massage or you could later 'punish' them with a spank for each wrong answer.

It can be great fun to do this game with food as you're playing with tastes, temperatures and textures all at the same time. Tease your partner with each bit of food as you feed them, kiss champagne into their mouth or lick up the bits around their lips. Jelly, ice cream, maraschino cherries, olives, honey, cookies, popcorn, melted chocolate – the possibilities are endless! If you need some inspiration, get onto YouTube and check out the famous food scene by the refrigerator in the film *9 1/2 Weeks.*

NIPPLE CLAMPS

Nipples are very sensitive and can be a great source of pleasure whether pinched, tweaked or sucked. And whilst most people think of nipple clamps as painful, some can be intensely pleasurable. Here are my top three picks for nips.

Clothes pegs: An inexpensive and surprisingly sexy toy is the humble wooden clothes peg. Go shopping and test a few on your finger and you'll see how widely they vary in the amount of tension they deliver.

***

My first time with clothes pegs

Funnily enough, I'd never used clothes pegs until I researched this book – I'd always been a bit scared of trying them as they look painful. But dedicated author that I am, I grabbed one off the washing line, nipped my nipple with it, and was surprised to find myself feeling rather horny! The feeling was even more pleasurable when I took the clothes peg off.

I discovered – all in the name of research, you understand – that the further up your nipple you put the clothes peg the more you spread the tension. Pull your nipple out and put the clamp close to its base and it delivers a very erotic feeling indeed. Put one right on the tip of your nipple, though, and it really hurts. Ouch!

***

Tweezer clamps: These are among my favourite nipple toys as I find they offer the lightest, most sensual feeling without any pain. They are simply a small pair of tweezers with a rubber ring around them that you can push up and down until the clamp pinches your nipple. Slip the ring further towards your nipple to intensify the feeling. What I really love, though, is that you can get tweezer clamps with bells on the end – great fun for role play!

Snake Bite Kit: People see opportunities for pleasure everywhere it seems, even in snake bite kits! Simply squeeze the air out of the rubber cylinder and attach it to your nipple. This draws blood into it, increasing its sensitivity and delivering a lovely rush.

Try attaching the cylinder to the clitoris. And wherever you put it, place a vibrator against it for a unique sensation.

HOW TO MAKE SEX ELECTRIC – LITERALLY!

Electro play, also known as e-stim or electro stimulation, is sensation play's best-kept secret. It involves applying electricity to the skin to produce a pleasurable, unusual feeling – and, frequently, intense hands-free orgasms.

Chiropractors and physiotherapists have long used electricity to contract and relax muscles as part of treatment, and the latest wave of electro play toys stimulate the nerves in the same way. I'd strongly recommend you choose one of the made-for-play electro kits on the market, rather than fiddling about with electricity to create your own device.

SAFETY FIRST! Electricity can kill so please follow the toy's instructions carefully. You want a rush of pleasure, not a rush to the emergency ward.

Out of the huge array of electro play devices out there, here are three favourites.

Electro insertables: These can be used vaginally or anally, producing a tingling electrical stimulus and feelings of intense pleasure that can lead to orgasm.

A kit consists of a power box, cables and an electrode, available in a variety of different diameters. You'll also need to buy batteries and, most importantly, conductive gel. The power box has an adjustable knob so you can deliver anything from a light tickle to a powerful driving pulse.

Reputable companies like E-stim Systems produce a range of safe made-for-play equipment that is well-priced, versatile and comes with a lifetime guarantee. If you're starting out, try the Intro2Electro For Her which you can buy online from E-stim Systems e-stim.co.uk.

Conductive rubber cock loops: These wonderful little devices are revolutionising electro cock play. You put the two soft, flexible rubber loops over the shaft of your lover's cock with some conducting gel, gently tighten them and then hook them up to the power box.

Sensations range from the gentlest buzz to a hard thrusting pulse, and the modes vary from soft and smooth to a spiky tingle. You can vary the intensity with the control box – and, yes, bring him to orgasm that way if you so intend!

I highly recommend the Intro2Electro For Him from E-Stim. If you want to combine it with the Intro2Electro for Her, described above, you can save money by choosing the Ultra Pack.

Neon wand: Similar to a violet wand, a neon wand gives a much milder sensation and is far less expensive. I find violet wands too intense, so unless that's what you're after, a neon wand is ideal while you're beginning your foray into electro play.

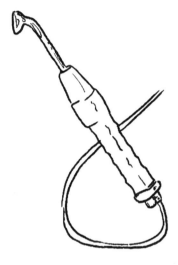

Neon Wand

The thrill of the neon wand is as much in its appearance and sound as the feeling it produces. The glass attachment at the end of it becomes charged with static electricity, which creates a cracking sound; and as it's held near the body, sparks jump to the skin. The feeling is interesting – you can enjoy anything from a warm tingle to a more intense sting.

Rather than using a continuous current as a power source, the neon wand discharges static electricity, which means you get a weaker charge. So unlike the two toys above, it's safe to use above the waist, even on nipples, and it doesn't need a conducting gel.

The wand comes with several attachments. The smaller the attachment, the more intense the feeling because electricity is distributed over a reduced area. It's mild enough to use on genitals but please don't insert it anywhere – the attachments are made of glass and you don't want them breaking! Again, you're playing with electricity so be sure to carefully follow the safety instructions, which includes taking off all metal jewellery.

Try Kinklab's Neon Wand Electro Sex Kit. Add to the fun by getting their Power Tripper accessory, which transforms your entire body into the conductor so you can use your own fingertips to send electrical tingles all over any part of your partner's body. Yes, with this toy it's possible to deliver literally electric oral sex!

> *My boyfriend ran his fingers up and down my arm and my skin began to tingle lightly with the buzz of electricity. It felt amazing and made me crave his electric touch all over my body! Then he ran his fingers up the back of my neck and into my hair. I was literally shaking. I thought if this is electro play, I want more of it.* – **Emma**

Neon wands are also great to use as part of role play. Whether you're playing mad scientist and victim, doctor and patient or doing an interrogation scene, the look, sound and feel of the device is really fun to play with. To find out where to buy this and all the toys listed in this book, download my free 'Secret Sex Toy Guide' at http://thekinkysexbook.com /secret-sex-toys/.

MAKING SENSE OF THE SENSES

The power of sensation play is in surrendering to your lover and enjoying the anticipation of their touch, of being denied or granted pleasure, which is extremely liberating. It can be a simple, sensual exploration or, as in the following scene, you can combine it with many other forms of play like Domination/submission or bondage. It's up to you how far you take it.

Sensory Deprivation

I am tied spread-eagled, wrists and ankles bound to the bedposts, under my Master's complete command. A hood blocks out all my vision and hearing. All I can sense is the beating of my own heart and the quickening of my breathing.

I wait for what seems an eternity, knowing he is enjoying watching me bound, helpless and aching for his touch. His fingers lightly graze the skin of my breasts and as I gasp in surprise, he pinches my nipples hard. I let out a whimper.

Now the wetness of his tongue is on my inner thigh, and I am powerless to prevent it. As he works his way up I quiver with desire. Every nerve of my body is focused on the sensation. He moves higher and higher, his mouth kissing my thighs teasingly, then nibbling, then licking. I am wet with longing but he will not give me what I want.

An icy burn hits my skin; I shiver as I feel the slickness of an ice cube dragged across my breasts. He knows I have no idea what is coming next. I am totally at his mercy. I love it when he teases me like this.

His fingers reach down and brush against my wet pussy. I feel the soft warmth of his tongue between my lips, slowly trailing up one and then the other. Tantalisingly, he slides his tongue ever so slightly inside. I thrust my hips up, yearning for him to fill me entirely. But again he stops before giving me what I want.

At last, I feel the chill of a smooth, round metal dildo being pushed into me, slowly, as I writhe in pleasure.

Then, without warning, a jolt of electricity. My muscles contract as involuntary spasms roll through me like little forced climaxes. I moan and buck in pleasure. An orgasm is building. He reads my responses expertly, lessening the intensity of the shocks to prevent me from coming. I so badly want to look into his eyes.

I feel the weight of him upon me now, and as if reading my mind he unlaces the hood and pulls it off completely. Looking into his eyes I feel like a gift being unwrapped, and I thirstily drink in the sight of him. His eyes are filled with lust for me and lust for the power he has over me.

"You look so helpless," he whispers, and kisses me tenderly. I want him so much.

"You've been a very good girl, haven't you?" he says.

"Yes Master."

"Do you think you've been a good enough girl to deserve Master's cock in your cunt?"

"Yes Master, please Master," I moan, aching for him.

Then slowly, teasingly, he eases his cock into me, his gaze so intense I can't look away. He slides his hand up the nape of my neck and grabs a fist full of hair. When he is all the way inside me he stays there, not moving. Totally controlled.

"Would you like Master to fuck you?" he asks, deep inside me but not moving. Still holding my hair, still forcing me to look into his eyes.

"Yes Master!" I whimper in reply.

"Are you sure you deserve it?"

"Yes Master!"

"Then beg me."

"Please Master fuck me!"

"Keep saying it."

"Please Master fuck me! Please Master fuck me!"

Gripping my hair tightly in his fist, he slowly moves, coming almost all the way out of me. Then teasingly, he slowly pushes into me again, filling me entirely. And he slow-fucks me, tantalisingly, holding eye contact, until he sees I'm on the verge of coming.

"Look me in the eye now and come for Master like a good girl," he says, slow-fucking me the entire time. He puts his hand over my mouth and I come, bucking against him, moaning into his hand, looking deeply into his eyes, feeling so proud to have obeyed him.

CHAPTER 7

THE SCIENCE OF SPANKING

Erotic spanking is one of the most common types of sex play out there: almost half of the population has indulged in it at some point. That's partly because the buttocks make up a pleasure-filled erogenous zone, full of sexual arousal nerves. Happily for us, each spank sends yummy waves of pleasure through to our genitals.

To suppress the pain of repeated smacks, spanking also triggers the release of endorphins, the happy brain chemicals that can quickly take you into the ecstatic depths of subspace.

And then there's the psychological side. Speaking from experience, there's nothing quite like the feeling of helplessness and vulnerability you get from being bent over your lover's lap, totally exposed with panties dropped and skirt lifted.

In this chapter you will discover:

- Tips to deliver a satisfying spanking
- The sweet spot
- The top five spanking positions
- How to spank your lover to orgasm
- How to use role play within a spanking scene

Spanking doesn't need to be about pain and punishment; it can be sensuous and erotic. It has long been used to alleviate anxiety, since the emotional release can be profound.

The science of spanking goes way beyond the physical – emotionally it can also be a hugely cathartic stress reliever. This was not lost on the Catholic Church, which in previous times saw to it that their priests spanked adult women after confession to assuage their sins. Lucky priests eh?

Modern scientific studies prove spanking to be therapeutic. A 2005 Russian study found the endorphins released in what they called 'whipping therapy' to be an effective treatment for alcohol and drug abuse, depression and even suicidal thoughts.

Today, many people continue to enjoy regular spankings just for the endorphin hit, which alleviates them from feelings of stress, depression or guilt. Some even use it to substitute medication.

From the spanker's point of view, the visual appearance of the spankee prostrate across their lap is a delicious turn-on. The feeling of control over your helpless lover is exciting, as is witnessing the lovely pink flush as it spreads across their cheeks.

Best of all, carefully landed strikes indirectly stimulate a woman's clitoris, so it's possible to bring her to orgasm just with spanking. And if you want to move on to sex, you'll be hard and ready from having her bare bottom squirming against you.

The origins of spanking

Spanking has a long history, though in times gone by it was dressed up as 'flagellation', conveniently considered rather wholesome by a succession of religions. The ancient Egyptian cult of Isis honoured the gods by whipping girls in the temple, whilst the ancient Greeks would strap a bride's bare bottom to encourage fertility.

Top marks, however, go to the 16th-century French tapestry I recently unearthed, which depicts a countryside scene with a man merrily spanking a buxom, bare-bottomed beauty over his knee. Roughly translated the accompanying text reads, "Since I have you bare-bottomed, plump shepherdess, you're going to get your backside smacked", to which the feisty shepherdess replies, "Gombault, you're not spanking hard enough. Besides, that's no way to spank a girl, with no promise of anything to follow!"

HOW DO I BRING UP SPANKING WITH MY LOVER?

Aside from the fantasy-sharing approach I described in Chapter 4, you could rent a movie like *Secretary* and then discuss the idea of trying something similar. Alternatively read some erotic spanking literature to your lover. You'll soon have an idea if it turns them on.

Or just hint flirtatiously. "Nice belt," you could say with a meaningful look, "you any good with it?" I've also tried the "I've been a very bad girl, I so deserve a spanking" when I've done something wrong. It seems to get the message across.

Role play is a great way to introduce spanking because it's fun and dispenses with inhibitions: it's not you who wants to spank her, it's that mean headmaster you're pretending to be! Playing a role allows you to say and do things you wouldn't normally, which is freeing.

Remember, plenty of men like to be spanked too: the same happy chemicals get released for both sexes. The descriptive sections of this chapter assume the man is the one spanking, but to reverse the roles, just swap the pronouns around.

There's a time for spanking and a time to refrain from spanking. Some guys will test you by throwing a little spank in during intercourse, which is a complete turn-off for me. It feels like a half-hearted effort, as though he's not confident enough to put me over his knee or talk to me about it. As far as I'm concerned, spanking feels so amazing that it should be a play activity we savour and enjoy, not just an after-thought. **– Angela**

WHERE DO I START?

The better you plan the scene the sexier it will be, so be sure to build anticipation in the lead-up. For example, what do you want your lover to wear? For a spanking scene white pop socks, a lift-able short flared skirt, suspenders, white panties, sexy lingerie or a full schoolgirl outfit all have their charms. Texting her beforehand to tell her exactly what to wear adds to the anticipation and builds desire.

There's no hurry. Take your time and savour every moment. Let your eyes slowly take her in top to toe after she arrives – intensely scrutinising her will intensify her excitement. You might order her to turn around, touch her toes or go and stand in the corner. Come up behind her and whisper into her ear that she's been a bad girl and let her protest that she hasn't.

It's often a big turn-on to punish her for a real-life misdemeanour, especially if it's a failing she's aware of like untidiness, drinking too much the night before or being late. The idea that you're reforming her can be very hot. Don't underestimate the importance of this lead-up. It can make or break your scene.

THE ART OF SPANKING

Much of spanking is science, but there's also an art to it. Without practice, few people grasp when and how to land the most satisfying smacks. But by following these 10 techniques and paying close attention to her feedback, you'll be well on your way to an orgasm-inducing spanking.

1. Get into position

You have two choices here: either calmly order her over to you and demand she assumes the position, or grab her and force her into it. Both variations work for different types of scene.

If you call her over, a "come here, Young Lady" or "over my knee. Now." works well. Scold her for her misdemeanour and order her to tell you why she's being spanked before you begin. Once you are satisfied, tell her to get into any of the spanking positions described later in this chapter.

Alternatively, simply beckon her over with a serious face and motion with your hand where you want her positioned. This is powerful as it demonstrates total control without having to say a word.

If you're grabbing her by force, fix her with a long, lustful look, suddenly grasp her by the hair and force her into position. She might struggle a little – you've got a safeword, right? Position her near a full-length mirror if you want her to witness her punishment.

2. Savour the anticipation

Once you have her there, take your time. She'll be wondering what you're going to do next and when. By now, her breathing might be quick and she may even be shaking with desire. Draw out this moment and you'll heighten the erotic anticipation.

Gently stroke her bottom. Enjoy the view and the feeling of control over her as she offers her behind to you. You might want to lift her skirt or lower her knickers, or order her to do the honours herself. Take your time and savour the experience. Use any trigger words you know work for her.

3. Focus on the sweet spot

Oh, the sweet spot – being spanked there really is very sweet indeed! The area covers the fleshy underside of the bottom, towards the centre, and the very upper inside thighs. Hit further up and it feels like having your lower back whacked, plus you risk hitting the easily-shattered tail bone; hit too far out to the sides of the buttocks and it just doesn't feel sexy. But the sweet spot, as Goldilocks says, is just right.

4. Warm up

A good spanking requires a warm-up. Start with light, rapid spanks and continue till the checks begin to blush. The spankee will get a lovely warm, tingling feeling in her posterior. Stop for a little, examine your handiwork and repeat the warm-up, this time slightly more firmly.

5. Enhance your hand technique

Spank rhythmically, keeping a steady pace without too much force: it's the number of spanks that counts, not the intensity. Alternate cheeks with each spank.

To start with, keep your hand rigid and use it like a paddle. Relax your wrist and slightly cup your hand. Later you can try spreading your fingers for more intensity.

6. Take a break

After the first set of spanks stop and caress her neck, pull her hair or play with her pussy. Check in by whispering into her ear a gentle "How're you doing?"

7. Continue

Once she's recovered, land 10 more spanks. As her buttocks flush you can go a little harder. You can also tell her to part her legs, then spread her buttocks with one hand and gently spank her pussy or anal area with three fingers.

8. Watch her body language

Is she bucking her bottom towards you (good) or pulling away (which could mean she's had enough)? Are her noises sounds of pleasure and release, or real pain? As always, stay alert to the signals she's giving you.

9. Make her come

Using good technique on the sweet spot alone can make some women climax. If that's what you're aiming for, pace things so you're saying her trigger words when she's nearing orgasm.

For others, varying a set of 10 spanks with clitoral stimulation while she spreads her legs works a treat. Reach down and tease her clitoris between spanking sets, keeping her on the edge for as long as you like, shifting between the pleasure of light clitoral stroking and the pain of a good, hard spanking. Before you know it she will be climaxing intensely.

If you don't want her to orgasm yet, watch her symptoms of arousal closely so you can judge when to move from spanking her to intercourse, or whichever type of play you want to continue to.

10. Give her aftercare

Let her lie there until she gains composure. Stroke or hold her close, gently comfort her and let her know she's forgiven for her bad behaviour. Aftercare is often the most intimate, bonding moment of the entire scene.

TOP FIVE SPANKING POSITIONS

Spanking can be done in the kitchen, the bedroom, outdoors, across the bonnet of the car – the options are endless! But wherever you choose, here's my run-down of the top five spanking positions.

1. Over the Knee (also known as OTK)

The position: Face down, over his lap while he sits on an armless chair. Either keep her legs together, whip up her skirt and pull down her knickers, or take her underwear completely off and order her to spread her legs so you can play with her naughty bits between spanking sets. You can wrap one leg around one of her legs to hold her in place and control kicking.

It's great because: It's the classic spanking stance; no other position provides as much closeness and skin-on-skin contact. The spanker gets a lovely view of a half-bent derrière conveniently within striking distance and the wonderful feeling of her body weight as she submits. Either command your spankee into the position or haul her into it (gravity is on your side).

Over the Knee (OTK)

Drawbacks: The spankee needs to support herself on her hands and toes, which gets tiring, and some say it's a distraction from the sensation. For others, balancing this way just adds to the sweetness of the humiliation.

Variations: Sit on the edge of the bed and angle her into it so her legs hang off the bed but her body is over your knees and across the bed. Alternatively, sit at the head of the bed and lean back against the headboard, lying her over your lap. This is a great position in which to grab her hair. Run your fingers up the nape of her neck and firmly grip her hair rather than actually tugging at it.

Tip: Different chair heights will lower or raise her bottom, both of which have their appeal. Experiment and see which you prefer.

2. Bent Over

The position: The spankee stands bent over with her hands on a bed, table, tree stump or pretty much anything else that's stable!

Bent Over

It's great because: Also a classic, it adds the opportunity to use longer implements as well as your hand. It's also perfect if you want to take things from spanking to rear-entry intercourse.

Drawbacks: There's no skin-on-skin contact as with OTK, which means it feels less intimate.

Variations: Try this position over something high like a kitchen counter top, so the spankee can support herself on her elbows.

3. Hands and Knees

The position: On hands and knees, doggie style.

Hands and Knees

It's great because: Most women look sexy in this position. It hides your tummy, raises your buttocks and makes your breasts look pert. You can use pretty much any implement and it's easy to move from spanking into doggie-style intercourse.

Drawbacks: Again, there's no skin-on-skin contact.

Variations: The spankee often ends up on their elbows, which raises the bottom.

4. Knees Up

The position: She lies on her back at the edge of the bed, knees lifted and legs spread. If you're keen on bondage you can tie her under each knee and fasten the rope at the bed legs so she can't close her legs. Tie her wrists so she can't move her hands to protect her smarting behind.

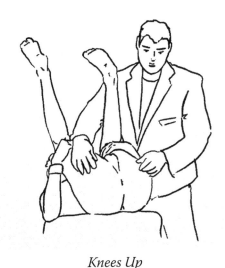

Knees Up

It's great because: This is as vulnerable as it gets; she is completely exposed and everything's on show, so it's wonderful if she enjoys feeling helpless and humiliated. It's one of the few stances where both of you can make eye contact, which is extremely hot and intimate during a spanking. It's perfect for delivering pussy spankings and you can easily move on to intercourse. So many options!

Drawbacks: It's difficult to hold for long periods as your hip flexor muscles tend to cramp up.

Variations: By keeping her legs together instead of spreading them, you can enjoy the visual titillation of seeing her panties around her knees. You can spank her for a while before removing her knickers and spreading her legs.

5. Bongo Drums

The position: The spanker sits on the edge of the bed with pillows behind his back for support. She faces away from him, face down, hands on the floor with her legs wrapped around his waist.

Bongo Drums

It's great because: He gets the visual thrill of her arse pertly presented for him high in the air. Plus easy access to her buttocks, anus and pussy and the bonus of using her bottom as a bongo drum with both hands! You can also use this position whilst having sex, though many find spanking and sex at the same time to be over-stimulating.

Drawbacks: It's often hard for her to maintain for a significant length of time, as her wrists are supporting her body weight.

Variations: If it's more comfortable, try this with the spanker sitting cross-legged.

As you can see from the scene below, role play is perfectly suited to spanking. You're not responsible for what that character wants because you're just playing a part, so you're free to explore.

Detention

I stumble into his house, clumsy and nervous, almost knocking a vase over as I throw my satchel to the ground. He is watching me closely.

"So careless," he shakes his head. He's standing by the door in his headmaster's gown impatiently checking his watch. His voice is stern. "You're late, Young Lady."

"Sorry," I mumble, stifling a girlish giggle. It feels like I'm channelling another me, the faintly rebellious teenager I never was. My own youth was spent studying for exams and in deep contemplation of profound life questions like how to save the planet. I was so serious, so shy, always such a good girl. But now I just feel naughty.

He towers above me – dark, powerful and intimidating in his sweeping black gown. I stand there awkwardly feeling so small and young next to him. It's the first time we've seen each other in the headmaster and school girl outfits we've prepared but both of us are too heavily in scene to admit the incredibly horny effect they have on us.

"And what's this?" he questions, pointing to my short skirt. "This is not school uniform and you know it." He shakes his head. "You have a lot to learn, Young Lady."

I hang my head in shame but I'm smirking a little.

"What's so funny?" he demands.

"Nothing Headmaster," I say, trying to wipe the smile off my face. It's liberating to feel this bad.

His voice is low and firm, the pupils of his eyes dilated in lust. "You won't be smiling when you see what I have in store for you." I love it when he tells me off. His voice is mild, understanding.

"Fortunately, Headmaster is here to correct and educate you. You know your grades are slipping. Your parents and I have agreed I should give you... special after-hours tuition. But first," he says mildly, pulling up a chair, "come and sit in my lap."

I obediently sit on his knee, and as I do I feel he's rock hard. He looks down at my legs and runs a finger lazily, proprietarily up the inside of my thigh, moaning as he lifts my short skirt. I feel a line is being crossed, but he's the one in charge so I obey. I'm panting hard. I know I should close my legs but somehow this feels too good. I feel wonderfully disobedient for enjoying his inappropriate attention.

"I think there's something you need to tell me," he murmurs softly into my ear.

I'm confused. "What, Headmaster?"

"You know what I'm talking about. I've seen you flirting with the boys at the comprehensive school down the road."

I stifle a giggle again. The comprehensive down the road. What a lovely touch.

"I'm sorry Headmaster. It won't happen again."

"I saw you lifting your skirt for them. Isn't that right?"

"Yes Headmaster," I'm flushing, hanging my head in embarrassment.

"You're a very bad girl. But fortunately for you, Headmaster is here to make you good again. So you need to be punished. Now get up."

I stand obediently.

"You've been a very bad girl and bad girls need to be taught a lesson. Now get over my knee."

My heart races as I do as he says, positioning myself in his lap with my arse high in the air. He lifts my schoolgirl skirt to discover a white, virginal pair of knickers. He drinks them in with his eyes and I know he loves them. He pushes them up between my cheeks to expose my bare, spankable arse. My face is flushed in shame. I so want him to touch me.

"You're going to take your punishment like a good girl aren't you?"

"Yes Headmaster," I whisper, writhing in anticipation. I can't wait for him to get started.

"Ten spanks for my bad little schoolgirl. Count them out."

The first smack hits my arse, hard. "One," I count, writhing and moaning at the impact. Within seconds the pain gives way to a rush of pleasure and arousal.

The second smack hits my other buttock. "Two!" I call out breathlessly.

The third smack is harder. "Three," I gasp in pleasure, pain and humiliation. Each spank sends shock waves through my pussy, drenching my pretty white knickers.

His commanding hand rains down again, strong and firm, giving me the discipline I know I so deserve. "Four," I moan, squirming against his hard cock. I know this is my punishment and I should not be enjoying it.

"Five!" I cry out, crumbling. It's borderline between pain and pleasure but he reads me perfectly and stops for a moment. He touches the wet gusset of my white panties, moaning, relishing having me in such an exposed position for him.

"Mmmm, you're all wet. I think my naughty little schoolgirl's enjoying this."

He crosses the boundary into complete inappropriateness as he slides his hand under my knickers, touching my pussy lips. I gasp, ashamed that he now knows quite how much I'm loving my punishment.

But he doesn't linger. With one swoop he's whisked my panties completely off and I'm there across his lap, my bare arse in the air, totally helpless and vulnerable for him. He takes his time to survey me. I can hear his breathing quicken.

"Spread your legs for me," he orders in a low, firm voice and of course, like a good girl I obey. He leans down to look between my legs, spreading my wet pussy lips and examining me closely. "Mmm, such a beautiful cunt," he says and my face flushes in shame as I moan under his humiliating gaze.

The sixth smack comes down, but this one hits my pussy. I gasp in shock. "Six!"

"That cunt needs punishing and disciplining," he states breezily. "Spread your legs apart as wide as they'll go now like a good girl."

Smacks seven and eight hit my pussy in quick succession and I count them out obediently, shock waves of pain and pleasure shooting through me. It's almost too much to bear.

"You need to be corrected so these last two are going to hurt. Do you understand?" he asks.

"Yes Headmaster," I reply, quivering in anticipation.

His spanks hit my arse. "Nine! Ten!" I cry out, writhing in pain and finally falling across him, almost sobbing with the sense of release that always comes from a good spanking.

CHAPTER 8

....

PUBLIC PLAY

The risk of getting caught, the spiking adrenaline, the racing of your heart – it feels so naughty to play in public places. The excitement of the event makes for a fun, urgent, super-hot experience, a one-off encounter never to be repeated. And the role playing possibilities are endless.

On the other hand, the very thing that makes public play so sexy – the chance of discovery – makes much of it risky and even illegal. Fortunately, however, there are more ways than you'd imagine to play in public without breaking the law. In this chapter, you'll discover how to:

- Give your lover an orgasm in public – without touching them
- Take sexy photos while you're out and about
- Have sex in public without getting caught
- Find ten great locations for public play
- Use role play to spice up any outing

HOW DO I BRING THIS UP WITH MY LOVER?

The anxiety associated with possibly getting caught fuels arousal, but it's a delicate balance: too much apprehension and you'll be turned off, just enough and it acts as an intense aphrodisiac. So when you raise the idea, it's important to reassure your lover that you want to do it safely, legally and without the risk of serving jail time! Plan the encounter well and above all, keep both of you safe.

Warning

Check out the nudity and obscenity laws in your area. No amount of fun is worth risking going to jail or having a criminal record. This chapter does not encourage you to break the law. Yes, the thrill of getting caught can be fun, but if someone sees you you're technically involving them in a sex act without their consent. This will land you in even more trouble if you happen to be spotted by a minor. Never do anything where you risk the chance of being spotted by someone who's underage.

WHERE DO I START?

Begin with less risky scenarios. Start experimenting in the car – you'll feel excitingly exposed but be safely in your getaway vehicle. It's a semi-private space and other drivers and pedestrians usually can't see what you're getting up to below the waist.

Drive somewhere secluded and tease your lover while you're parked, or if you're sure you're alone, get out and spank them over the boot of the car. If you're at the wheel, order your lover to play with themselves but tell them to stop just before orgasm. You can get them to do this over and over again, raising their frustration level until you either get home and do the deed or finally let them come in the car. Whatever happens though, keep your eyes on the road while you're driving!

Combining a public scenario with Domination/ submission techniques (which you'll discover in Chapter 9) creates an erotic sense of vulnerability, as you can see here.

In the Car

As I walk towards the car I can feel my heart beat fast with nervous anticipation. The windows may be tinted but I still feel his eyes on me. His gaze is so palpable I can hardly walk straight. I almost trip on my high heels; I must look so clumsy. I'm in between worlds, caught in the space that separates the everyday of my life and the fantasy world we create together. It's physically disorienting.

I open the car door and flash him a huge grin, attempting to mask my awkwardness. Head cocked to the side with a slight smile, he says a casual hello. His eyes travel slowly down my body mentally undressing me, but with such nonchalant detachment that I'm fumbling with my seatbelt like a fool. He is totally in control.

I babble about my day as I strap myself in, not meeting his eye. When I eventually finish I look at him and he's holding back a laugh, so amused at my discomfort. I know he gets off on seeing how nervous he makes me.

He ignores everything I've said and makes no move to start the car. "Mmmmmm," he purrs languidly, his eyes trailing hungrily over my body. "You wore just what I told you to."

I'm wearing a knee-length, pretty little black fitted dress with high heels and stockings, no panties. Just as instructed. I am a present for him, packaged up just the way he likes me.

But I'm nervous. We are not yet in scene. I'm fighting for my power, for control of the conversation, whilst also deeply wanting to give it up. I am still me, not yet his slut.

He can see it, too. He knows how my mind works. He knows I like to control conversations with my questions, he knows I can beat him in any argument. But he also knows I yearn deeply to submit to him. And that no one else has quite his aura of power and command – of cool, calm control. His kinky imagination, his ability to get into my head and push my buttons. He knows he is the only man who's ever really seen the whole person I am, both in my power and wholly, gloriously stripped of it.

He looks at me till I meet his eye apprehensively, then pauses.

"Master has a present for his slut," he says. Excitement ripples through me and I smile.

"What is it?" I giggle. We don't do flowers and chocolates, we have other ways of showing our feelings.

"These," he says, casually tossing a pair of extendable handcuffs into his hands. I gasp. He knows I am waiting to see how he will use them.

He fixes me with his Dom look – dark, cruel, commanding. I recognise it well: it's the look that tells me in no uncertain terms that I am to do exactly what he says. And instantly I'm under his spell.

"Put your hands behind the seat, Slut. I'm going to cuff you," he says.

"Yes Master," I say and obey without question. He restrains my hands behind the seat. My shoulder blades squeeze together, my breasts forced forward as though presented to him. I hear the handcuffs click as the cold steel grips my wrists. I struggle a little, feeling the welcome pinch against my skin. The tightness is liberating. Finally I can let go.

"Now..." he says pausing, running his eyes over me again like he owns me. I feel so degraded, so at his disposal. It's an intensely exciting feeling to be wanted this much, to be scrutinised this closely. I know he is toying with me.

He leans in close to me, tutting gently. I feel his warm breath on my neck.

"Slut has forgotten her training," he whispers disapprovingly.

"Have I?" I whisper back all flustered, ashamed to have failed him.

He reaches over and runs his fingertips slowly from my knee to my thigh, moaning a little as he feels the smoothness of my sheer stockings beneath his touch, knowing I am powerless to prevent him doing whatever he desires. He is teasing himself with me. Devouring me slowly, drawing out the thrill of having me as his own for these brief few hours we have together.

"Such a bad girl. You know the rules," he says, meeting my gaze. "Slut's legs are always spread for Master and her cunt is always wet."

Gasping at my carelessness, I immediately spread my legs. He slides his hand up slowly, brushing his fingers nonchalantly against my soaking cunt. He moans again and sucks his fingers, pleased. He is still teasing himself with me. I love being his plaything.

> Suddenly he breaks away and turns the key in the ignition. As he drives I sit there with my hands cuffed behind the seat, my legs spread and my pussy soaking, completely at his mercy. We stop at a red light and, as casually as if he were twiddling with the dial of his radio, he leans over to lightly tease my soaking pussy.

Public play does not need to lead to orgasm; in fact, often it's the very impossibility of sex that's so enticing. It gives you the chance to tease your lover all day long, drawing out the sense of anticipation which so often fuels great sex. A little whispered word here, a discreet fondle there, can be intensely erotic if drawn out over a long period.

Putting one of you in control for the evening can be fun, too. If you're out to dinner, once you've ordered your meals, tell your lover to go to the restroom, remove their underwear and masturbate till just before orgasm before returning. Then tease them throughout the meal by telling them all the things you have planned for them when you get back. By the time you get home you'll be hot for each other.

GIVE YOUR LOVER AN ORGASM IN PUBLIC WITHOUT TOUCHING THEM

It's the technological advance that's changing the world: the remote control vibrator! Just slip the device inside yourself and have your lover use the discreet control device to stimulate you when you're out and about.

I've seen men fall over themselves to take a girl shopping (yes, shopping!) just for an excuse to use one of these little modern-day miracles. Since it's silent and worn internally, it's impossible for anyone to notice it, so you can't get arrested. Only you and your lover know your naughty little secret.

It can be the perfect tease, too: by carefully watching her reactions you can take a woman right to the brink of orgasm and then switch the device off. Combine it with a little dirty talk whispered into her ear or give her tasks to perform in order for you to turn it back on again. And girls, handing your partner the remote control half way through the entrées is sure to spice up that romantic dinner!

> *My boyfriend waited till I went up to the sales counter, and just as I began talking to the shop assistant he turned the remote control vibrator on. I was so surprised I let out a little gasp! The sales assistant had no idea what was happening and she asked me if I was OK. I just smiled and nodded. As he turned the vibrations up I actually had to hold on to the counter to be able to stand! After a few minutes of high speed my panties were soaking and I couldn't help letting out a few moans.* **– Annabel**

You can perk up pretty much any everyday outing with a remote control sex toy. Take it to the cinema, out to a party or even a posh black-tie event. And did I mention they can be used on men too? The best quality ones are made for vaginal or anal insertion.

The most advanced one on the market is the Lyla 2, part of the luxurious Lelo range. It looks like a piece of art and is made of body-safe silicone with a smooth, velvety feel to it, so it's a perfectly discreet addition to your handbag. It's waterproof and rechargeable, has a large wireless range and gives high intensity, silent vibration with both pulsating and vibrating functions. This is one toy you'll get endless enjoyment from. To find out where to buy it, and all the sex toys in this book at a great price, go to www.thekinkysexbook.com /secret-sex-toys.

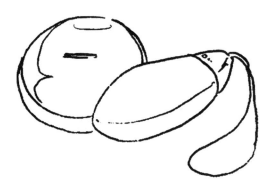

The Lyla 2 Remote Control Toy

What's the naughtiest place you've ever used a remote control vibrator?

That's the question I posed to a group of remote control vibrator fans, and here's what they said.

"They're great fun at a museum or public library."

"At an open house day for a house sale, just as she asked the agent a question about the heating system."

"I used one at my cousin's wedding a year ago, during the ceremony."

"I like using it in a restaurant while she's ordering food."

"At her family reunion."

"We use ours at church – only God knows! It certainly helps keep Sunday mornings interesting."

"In class at university."

"On the bus."

And my personal favourite:

"I had my girlfriend squirming in her seat on a six-hour flight because she knew, every time the 'fasten seat-belts' light went on, she'd get a zap until it went off again. Halfway through the flight I 'accidentally' dropped the remote and pretended 'somebody who must have found it' was fiddling with it, but it was me all along."

TAKING SEXY PHOTOS IN PUBLIC PLACES

If you did the secret sexual personality quiz in part I and discovered you're a bit of a voyeur or exhibitionist, this one's for you.

Armed just with a camera, embark on a field trip with a twist. The idea is for one of you to quickly flash a part of your body – genitals, nipples, bottom – while the other takes a photo. Best of all, you'll have keepsakes to remember your escapade by.

Try photographing your partner in a variety of places like a deserted park, phone booth, riding down an escalator, sitting on some stairs or in a hotel bathroom. As always, be sure no one sees you: you're posing for your partner's eyes only. In particular, be careful of using a flash at night as that's sure to attract attention.

HOW TO HAVE PUBLIC SEX WITHOUT GETTING CAUGHT

As you can see there's so much fun to be had without actually having sex in public. But if that's what you want to do, here's how to minimise your chances of getting caught.

Seek out secluded locations and scope out the scene of the crime beforehand. Visit the spot once or several times at the same time of day or night when you're planning your rendezvous to get an idea of how high your chances are of getting caught – and if it looks likely, choose somewhere else.

Identify anywhere you can duck for cover if you're discovered, think of ways to mask what you're doing, and have a story at the ready to use if you do get caught.

Having sex fully clothed is not only a turn-on but it's easier to make a fast escape if you're discovered, so dress for easy access. Ladies, try wearing a skirt or dress with no panties, no bra, a blouse with buttons and perhaps stockings and suspenders. Gentlemen, wear boxer shorts with an open fly.

Oral sex is a perfect choice as you don't need to remove much clothing and one of you can be on the lookout.

Masturbating each other makes you feel like naughty teenagers, and you don't have to take any clothes off so it's perfect for a quick getaway. Penetrative sex is trickier, but with the right clothes you can look as though you're just standing very close.

TOP TEN LOCATIONS FOR PUBLIC PLAY

Where to go? So many options! Look around for locations and you'll begin to see more and more opportunities. Here are my top ten ideas to get you started.

- Against the windows in a top-floor hotel room
- In a forest, sheltered by trees
- On a rooftop
- In the restroom of a posh hotel
- On a deserted beach
- In a national park at night
- On a hotel balcony
- In an abandoned warehouse
- In the sea
- In your own backyard

USE ROLE PLAY TO SPICE UP ANY PUBLIC OUTING

If you're planning a little role play, it's fun to begin your encounter in a public place rather than the bedroom. If you strut into that bar behaving like the sexy stranger you're pretending to be, no one but the two of you will know you're not really meeting for the first time.

Dressing in role can be electrifying, as you'll be the only ones who know you're not really who you appear to be. When you look and behave like a school teacher, photographer or businessman, why wouldn't strangers on the street believe you are one?

As we've seen, your mind is your biggest erotic asset. Bringing your roles into the outside world can pull you deeper into the fantasy than you would be if you began the scene alone at home. This builds desire and brings a super-hot feeling of novelty to the occasion: this may not actually be the first time you've had sex, but it is for your characters.

There's more about role play in Chapter 11, but for now just be aware that some roles lend themselves to public play more than others. Police officers don't take kindly to being imitated, and though doctors and nurses can be sexy, you don't want to be called on to provide medical attention!

Whether you indulge in role play or not, public play has the potential to turn just about any mundane outing into a sexy little escapade. Sharing a naughty secret that only the two of you know about makes everything feel different.

Fast Food

No one on the busy street knows our secret.

I teeter on ridiculously high heels as I walk down the street beside him. Though we're in public, everyone else fades away. It amazes me that people can pass us by without seeing the electric charge resonating between us. How can they not notice?

No one has a clue we're in scene – that at this moment I am his property, to do with what he will. And he's taking full advantage.

He's picked every item of clothing I'm wearing and ordered me to put a sex toy in my pussy – two shiny, weighted round balls, attached to each other by a string. I've not been permitted to wear knickers so I need to use all my muscles to hold them inside me as we walk down the street to the takeaway place. I can only take small steps.

I am blushing and of course, he's loving every second of this. He hangs back for me, smiling, relishing my discomfort and vulnerability.

We step into the take-away place and I whisper to him, "What if it comes out here and shoots onto the floor? I would be so embarrassed!"

"It won't," he responds, amused.

"But what if it does?"

He smiles at me and draws close to my ear. "Then I'll make you pick it up," he whispers with a wink, and walks up to the counter to order.

CHAPTER 9

·····················

DOMINATION/SUBMISSION

However politically correct we try to be, the reality is that power dynamics do exist in our world. Pretty much anything we do sexually involves one person doing something to the other. Erotic power exchange celebrates that inequality and makes it OK for us to play with it in a safe, consensual way.

Domination/submission (D/s) is a kind of role play where you act out a fantasy that involves taking or giving up power, using things like bondage, teasing and commands. It's fun, it's hot, it forms a powerful connection – and it's an exhilarating way to explore all sorts of fantasies.

Many of the scenes described in this book are examples of D/s. This chapter gives you a deeper insight into what it is, why you might enjoy dominating or submitting, and how to do it.

In this chapter we'll look at:

- Domination/submission – what's in it for you?
- The euphoric high of subspace and how to achieve it
- How to tell if you're a Dom(me), sub or switch
- Common myths about erotic power exchange
- The fine art of domination
- How to take things further

HOW DO I BRING THIS UP WITH MY LOVER?

Try the 'sexy – or not?' game in Chapter 3 for a flirtatious, low-pressure way to broach the subject. You could also say you've done this fun sex test, would they like to try it? Then use the online quiz at thekinkysexbook.com to discover whether they have submissive or dominant tendencies.

There's plenty of erotic literature around that deals with themes of Domination/submission. The best-known, of course, is *Fifty Shades of Grey*. Ask if they've read it, and if so what did they think? Alternatively you could read bits of erotic literature to your lover, even if you do it only as a joke. Admit you're getting a little turned on by what you're reading and see how they respond.

SUBMITTING – WHAT'S IN IT FOR A GUY?

Many men have submissive fantasies – according to some sources up to 50% of the male population, though stats like these are impossible to prove. Perhaps that's because they get tired of the pressure to sexually perform, often with a lot of guesswork and little feedback from women.

Then there are alpha males, who often just want a break from always calling the shots. They want to tip the balance of power in the opposite direction and be released from responsibility, at least for a while. The fantasy of submitting to a powerful woman is so common it has a name: Femdom, also known as female dominance or female supremacy, so I've devoted a whole chapter to it later on.

SUBMITTING – WHAT'S IN IT FOR A GIRL?

These days many women's lives revolve around control. They have senior positions at work, run the household and co-ordinate their kids' social calendars, and quite frankly it all gets rather exhausting. People forget that being in control is often something you do out of necessity, not choice. Some women love to be released from the pressure of taking control, and relish the feeling of being passionately desired by a lover who just has to have them.

Ever been whisked away on a date where your partner has planned and booked all sorts of exciting activities he knew you'd love? Not only is it romantic, it's an incredibly freeing experience to trust someone enough to let go and just enjoy the occasion. That's what submitting's like – including the romantic part. And that's without even touching on the intoxicating natural high you get from being in 'subspace'.

I find being challenged and humiliated hot. Without being big headed, in my day-to-day life I can pretty much handle whatever the universe throws at me, so being on the back foot (although not passive, another misconception of what being submissive means) and reacting often brings about an adrenaline high in its own right. Like sky diving but with more nakedness and no plummeting to the ground.

– Sophie Morgan,
best-selling author of *Diary of a Submissive*

WHAT'S IN IT FOR THE DOMINANT?

You get a huge power rush when you dominate. Life can be unpredictable, but dominating puts you in the driver's seat – at least for a while. Perhaps you have occasional fears of being disrespected or just want to feel admired? Well, wielding power in a scene helps you transcend those fears and feel the full rush of confidence. You're playing with someone who craves deeply to serve and obey your every command, which is a big kick.

The experience of dominating shows you there's nothing wrong with power so long as it's used wisely and consensually. It also demonstrates that with power comes responsibility, which in this case involves listening carefully to your submissive and their wants and needs before, during and after a scene so you can take them into states of unparalleled bliss.

True power is caring, attentive and protective just as it is strong, decisive and controlled. By listening intently and delivering an experience that your lover deeply enjoys, you build trust, closeness and a confidence in your own abilities, which often rubs off onto other parts of your life.

WHAT IS SUBSPACE?

Sometimes, when you hand over control to someone you trust completely, you drop into a trance-like state, a natural high called subspace.

It's much like a hypnotic trance, characterised by narrowly focused attention. Pleasure/pain play releases endorphins, which produce similar effects to morphine. This puts you in a euphoric, floaty state where time and space seem to disappear, and nothing exists but the two of you and the sensations. Again, it's very romantic to give or receive such an incredible experience.

Some people who reach such heights of ecstasy become incoherent, making safewords useless, so it's important to monitor your lover carefully and wind down the scene slowly.

> *The first time I ever submitted, I plummeted so deeply into subspace that I was floating for two days afterwards. The irony was that giving up control gave me such a lasting feeling of freedom and total omnipotence! Nothing and no one could rattle, annoy or scare me – I just had this feeling of deep bliss and an inner well of confidence and belief in myself.* **– Peta**

IS THERE SUCH A THING AS DOMSPACE?

Yes there is, but it isn't so well documented as subspace. Domspace feels like a tremendous rush of power, an intoxicating, god-like sense of omnipotence. Totally gratifying your partner and seeing the look on their face as you take them deep into the ecstasy of subspace gives you an incredible buzz. You feel desired and needed, and there's a huge ego boost in giving your lover what he or she wants.

HOW DO I KNOW IF I'M A DOM(ME) OR A SUB?

Don't get too caught up in labels, it's more about the type of role you prefer to play. Some people like to dominate, some like to submit – and some enjoy switching between the two depending on their mood, so they're called 'switches'. Other people just aren't into power exchange at all, but still enjoy giving and receiving sensation. So what are you?

Have you ever fantasised about being bound and helpless while your lover did all sorts of illicit things to you? Or telling your partner what to do as they fulfil your every command? Have a look at the role play examples in Chapter 11 and get a feel for if you see yourself in the dominant or submissive role, or if you even have any preference at all.

Many people are introduced to power play by a new lover and discover that a whole world of turn-ons suddenly opens up. The fact is that sometimes the only way to find out if something appeals is to try it. You never know what might turn you on, and if it's not your thing you don't need to do it again – so what's the harm?

TOP SEVEN MYTHS ABOUT DOMINATION/SUBMISSION

People often have misguided beliefs about what D/s is, so before we get to the how-to's let's explode some common misconceptions.

Myth No. 1: Domination/submission is a form of abuse.

Hitting someone does not mean you're hurting them. Spanking or even flogging is the same as anything: some people enjoy the sensation, some don't. I personally can't stand the feeling of someone else cutting and filing my fingernails, but I would hardly label manicurists abusers!

An abuser violates consent, caring nothing for the feelings, needs or wants of their victim – whereas a Dominant acts *with* consent, and cares *only* for the feelings, needs and desires of their lover. In the dominant role, you create a situation where you can both explore the submissive's fantasies.

Good Dominants are caring: they're driven to please their lover and spend a great deal of time discovering their turn-ons and creating a deeply pleasurable scene. This makes them highly in tune with their lover's feelings, whereas abusers care about only their own. The aim for the Dominant is usually to get pleasure from seeing the *submissive* receive pleasure.

The deep secret behind D/s is that the master is really the slave, and the slave is the master. Contrary to appearances, it's the submissive who's in control: they set the limits (the things that can and can't be done) and they can use a safeword to stop the scene at any point. In contrast, *an abuse victim does not get to say no.*

> *Many years ago, I read Stephen King's novella* Apt Pupil *and saw a bit too much of myself in there, and ended up in tears, haunted by the idea that I could be similarly*

seduced by the evil allure of raw power. My darling wife said, "Yes Roger, there are bad people who want to torture people to death, but what you want to do is torture me until I have an **orgasm**." And it was true. And I've been pretty comfortable with my unpolitically correct sexual identity since that moment. **– Roger**

Myth No. 2: People who practise Domination/submission are sick.

For millennia we've attacked people who are different from us, whether by burning them at the stake or relegating them to the *Diagnostic and Statistical Manual of Mental Disorders*, which at one point listed both gay people and kinky folk. But according to research published in May 2013 in the *Journal of Sexual Medicine*, people who are into erotic power exchange may actually be more psychologically healthy than those who aren't.

The study, which surveyed 902 people who liked BDSM and 434 who preferred things vanilla, asked questions which shed light on people's personalities, well-being, sensitivity to rejection and style of attachment in relationships. The participants weren't informed of the study's purpose.

Kinky people scored higher on indicators of mental health than those who liked things more vanilla. They were found to be less neurotic, more open, more secure in their relationships and to have better overall well-being. But why?

According to the study's author, psychologist Andreas Wismeijer, one reason could be that, whether dominant or submissive, people who practise erotic power exchange tend to be more aware of and communicative of their sexual needs.

That said, the results weren't definitive. Ultimately the study concluded that kinky people "either did not differ from the general population and if they differed, they always differed in the more favourable direction." In short, people who practise Domination/submission are not 'sick', and may even be more mentally healthy than those who don't.

Myth No. 3: Submissives are former victims of child sexual abuse.

Not true. Most submissives, including myself, grew up in loving homes with great parents and no history of childhood trauma. Personally, the closest I got to even being spanked was a light clip on the bottom perhaps twice in my life. People who enjoy D/s generally weren't abused, because victims of abuse don't tend to get turned on by giving someone power over them.

Sadly however, approximately one in three women and one in seven men have endured the dreadful trauma of child sexual abuse. Given these numbers, a high percentage of any group – redheads, BMW drivers, office workers – will have suffered abuse. But there's zero evidence to suggest the figures are higher for those who are into D/s.

Myth No. 4: Men are Doms and women are subs.

The truth is, both men and women can be Dominants (men are known as Doms, women as Dommes), or subs, or switches. And if you think submission is a relic from our misogynistic past, consider this: there seem to be substantially more male subs out there than female ones. That's why I've dedicated the whole of chapter 12 to what's popularly known as Femdom (female domination).

Myth No. 5: If you're dominant in life, you're dominant in bed.

Being a Dominant doesn't mean you're going to be a dynamic go-getter in your day-to-day life, and being a submissive doesn't make you a doormat.

Often, in fact, it's the reverse: we find an outlet sexually for the things we don't get the chance to experience in life. So we may enjoy submitting as a way of releasing ourselves from the heavy burden of a high-responsibility job, or be inclined to dominate if we feel we don't have much control in our lives.

But it isn't that simple either. There is no sure-fire way of knowing what someone's preference is without taking the time to get to know their sexual personality. Just as we are a different person at work from who we are at home, we're often quite another person in the bedroom from who we are socially.

Myth No. 6: You can change your submissive lover into a Dominant.

No you can't! You can no more convert a submissive into a Dominant (or vice versa) than you can turn a gay person straight.

Sadly, in my experience many couples stay married for years, but are unable to explore their desires with each other since both are either submissive or dominant. At the time you get together, neither of you has the knowledge or vocabulary to understand and communicate the fact that you are simply the same jigsaw piece, so how could you ever fit together?

Compatibility is important, so find out your lover's sexual personality early on. That said, our sexual interests do evolve with time and experience. If you or your partner is a switch, there's hope.

Some switches alternate fairly easily between dominating and submitting whilst others switch only in trusting relationships, seeing themselves perhaps as dominant 90% of the time. It's entirely possible to take someone who's 90% Dom, 10% sub and stretch their boundaries until they become perhaps 80% Dom, 20% sub. But again, that's only if they want that for themselves. You can't force them.

Myth No. 7: If you start exploring Domination/ submission, you'll never stop.

Some people are worried that if they start down the path of erotic power exchange there's no way back. But that's not the case.

The reason mainstream sex is referred to as 'vanilla' is that there's more than one flavour out there to taste. Just because you feel like raspberry ripple today doesn't mean you won't feel like vanilla tomorrow. Domination/submission is just one more delicious flavour to add to your menu. After all, if you already enjoy 'normal' sex (whatever that means to you), why would you suddenly go off it?

THE FINE ART OF DOMINATION

Dominating isn't just about knowing your knots, having fancy toys or bossing someone around. The key thing that makes you a good Dominant is getting into the headspace of your lover: communicating openly, sharing fantasies and building trust, respect and confidence. So before we get on to what to do, let's talk about something even more important: how to do it.

The top five traits of a Dominant

To relax and surrender, your lover needs to be able to explore his or her feelings with a responsibility-free mind-set. To do that, they need to be confident that you'll take care of them within the scene, and in particular that you:

1. Have a solid, unshakable respect for them

2. Have empathy for their feelings and have their best interests at heart

3. Will take charge of any situation that arises, such as their sister who still has a key walking in

4. Possess the level of skill, whether in bondage, cropping, electro play or anything else, to play safely

5. Will look after them when the scene has ended and give them proper aftercare

Your biggest asset as a Dominant is your self-confidence. If things don't go perfectly, that's OK; what's important is the way you deal with the situation. A Dominant who

> handles mishaps with a cool, calm air of confidence and control is sexy as hell. You're playing a role so project a sense of assurance, even if you don't feel it.

Have a pre-scene chat

In the dominant role, you're like a film director: you control how the action unfolds. But you want your movie to be a box office hit, so you'll need to discover as much as possible about what your 'audience' wants, too, which means planning your encounter according to your lover's fantasies.

There's the physical side of things as well. So your partner says she likes it rough, but how rough exactly? Talking beforehand lets you gauge things like this. It's also vital to know what your lover's limits are and to establish a safeword. Remember, Dominants also have their limits – and if you're uncomfortable with something, you get to safeword too!

Step into your power

To pull off the role of Dominant, it's vital for you to get in touch with your own power. This is about feeling a sense of authority – sensing, for example, the rush of control that comes with the idea that you could do anything to your lover when you have them tied up. Once you connect with that inner power, the role will come easily.

Harness the element of surprise

Ever watched a thriller with a scary bit that made you jump? Your heart starts racing, the adrenaline's pumping and you're entirely in the moment. You can use the same sense of apprehension, surprise and unpredictability in your play. The scenes described in this book give you plenty of ideas for how to do this.

Go slowly

Don't try to do everything at once. Again, it's better to have finished a scene thinking you could have done more than feeling you've gone too far.

Talk to each other afterwards

Once the scene's over, have a conversation to see what you both liked best and what you'd like to do differently next time. This is the key technique to keep your scenes getting hotter.

Why eye contact is your most important tool

Steely, cold, calm, in control – there's nothing more thrilling to a submissive than locking eyes with that dominant gaze. But why is it so powerful?

Researchers believe eye contact is fundamental to establishing the social hierarchy. Leaders use eye contact to control and dominate, even in the workplace, where it's believed subconscious stare-downs with our co-workers decide our eventual position in the company.

Numerous studies show that with good eye contact you're perceived as more attractive, skilled, sincere, confident, powerful and emotionally stable – all qualities of a good Dominant. You're also seen as more trustworthy: your inner emotions are often revealed by your eyes. Most importantly of all, good eye contact shows your lover you're giving them your complete, undivided attention, which is vital to any good scene.

HUMILIATION PLAY

"My girlfriend wants me to call her a dirty little slut when we have sex," said a friend of mine recently, shifting uncomfortably in his seat. "Surely that's disrespectful! How can I call her degrading names when I worship the ground she walks on?"

"Some women don't want to be worshipped the whole time," I replied. "It's cold and lonely up there on that pedestal."

The thing my friend was missing was the concept of consent. If a woman wants to be bossed around or tied up, that's her choice. But if a man assumes he can tell *all* women what to do, that's chauvinistic – and, most importantly, non-consensual.

In fact, those who enjoy erotic humiliation usually have cast-iron egos. We spend a lot of our lives making the right impression and presenting ourselves in the best light, and it gets tiring. We fear being humiliated or degraded – yet in a safe, consensual context, what we're afraid of often becomes a huge turn-on. It allows you to let go for a while, to fall and let someone you trust catch you.

Think of a time when you've broken down in tears in front of someone. Perhaps you felt a deeper bond with them because they were there for you at that moment.

Humiliation play works in a similar way: it creates that same sense of intimate bonding and vulnerability, but without the trauma. For a short time, you become an extension of your lover's will, allowing you to feel your own raw vulnerability. It's liberating.

> *The most freeing moment of my life took place when my ex-boyfriend put me in subspace. I felt entirely ego-less: for that time I no longer belonged to me, I belonged to him. Submitting gives me the most amazing euphoria – no drug I've ever tried compares. It's incredible that so many people live their lives without experiencing the natural highs our bodies are capable of.* **– Joanna**

In essence, D/s is about playing a role, and if the love of your life wants you to call her a whore, that's OK, because you're doing it within the scene with the intention of exciting her. Say it in front of her parents, however, and that's another matter! It's all about context.

Turning your lover on with humiliating talk doesn't make you disrespectful or evil, it just means you enjoy creating an arousing situation. In reality, you may think she's the most admirable person in the world – and playing a role for a few hours won't change that, any more than an actor playing a serial killer would be inclined to go on a killing spree.

SAFETY FIRST! As a Dominant, the first thing you need to be in control of is yourself. That means be rough but not too rough; you never want to take things too far. Your lover is in your care and your aim is to give pleasure, not to cause damage. Different people have different limits but no one should get hurt. For example, there's a difference between pinning someone down to restrain them and putting all your weight on their wrists so that you injure them. Know your lover's limits and respect them.

TOP TEN DOMINATION TECHNIQUES

Often D/s requires no tools, toys, costumes or props; it's the psychological control that's most exciting. Here are my top ten turn-ons which – along with a little dirty talk and with or without things like spanking and perhaps a little pain play – can take your lover deep into the ecstasy of subspace.

1. Eye control

Simple but incredibly powerful. Order your lover to be waiting for you on their knees with their eyes cast down at the floor, and make it clear that they're not allowed to look at you until you give permission. Draw out the tension by examining them from different angles, perhaps describing what you see.

2. Commands

Anyone can tell someone what to do but there's more to dominating than that. Giving commands is fun because within your lover's limits, he or she is compelled to obey. When you take control of your lover with your words, and see them willingly relinquish themselves to you, orders like "Kneel" or "Don't move" become a kind of verbal bondage.

For example, if you order her to slowly strip naked, spread her legs and masturbate for your amusement, she has to do it. If you command him to kneel before you with his hands behind his back and bring you to orgasm with his tongue, he'll do as he's told. If you tell her to pose in various ways while you take pictures, she must obey. You can see how much fun there is to be had here!

3. Speech control

If you've never had someone withhold your right to speak, you can't imagine how powerful this is. Tell your lover they aren't allowed to speak until you grant them permission or they'll be punished. When it was first done to me I realised just how much, as a woman, I depend on speech to control situations – especially since I'm not particularly strong physically.

4. Hair-pulling

Whether you're a guy or a girl, having your hair passionately pulled has a profound psychological effect. But be careful not to yank. Run your fingers up the nape of your lover's neck, grab a large fistful of hair and control their head with your handhold. You can grip your lover's hair during penetration, whilst they give you oral sex or, if you're discreet, when kissing them in public.

5. Face slapping

This can be incredibly hot for the submissive, especially if you do it to punish them for getting something wrong. For maximum effect, make sure it comes as a surprise. Having your face slapped can be a hard limit for some, so check during negotiation.

*When my girlfriend told me she liked rough sex, I happily obliged, but after the first couple of times I started feeling uncomfortable. I was raised by a single mum and grew up with two older sisters and a lifelong respect for women. So I struggled to give her what she wanted. Still, she kept asking me to be rougher. Slapping her in the face while we were having sex made me feel like a monster, until I saw how wet it made her! Now I realise that giving her what she wants **is** respecting her – and making her multi-orgasmic is pretty fun for me too! – **James***

6. Forced oral

Having your mouth used for your lover's pleasure feels gloriously humiliating. If you're a woman, you can just tie your lover down to the bed and sit on their face. If you're a man, grab her by the hair and hold eye contact with her as you force your cock into her mouth, ordering her to suck it. If you think she'll like it, push yourself to the back of her mouth. Always be sure your lover can breathe.

A posture collar holds your lover's head firmly in place, giving them an upward, attentive look and, as one toy company puts it, making them perfectly available for 'oral mounting'! Wearing a posture collar feels wonderfully submissive and snugly restraining. If it has an eyelet, attach a collar and leash and pull on it as you enter his or her mouth.

Posture Collar

7. Gagging

Restrict your lover's speech without totally eliminating their ability to make noise. Many submissives get erotic pleasure from being reduced to taking orders without being able to respond in any sensical sort of way. To nod, shake your head or speak gibberish becomes the submissive's only means of communication, which reduces them to a function of their Dominant's pleasure, an intensely liberating feeling.

When it comes to choosing a gag, a ball gag is a good toy to start with. Make sure you choose one that's the right size for your lover's mouth. Be aware, too, that gagging comes with risks. Watch your lover carefully at all times so they can breathe, and give them a 'safe signal' (perhaps a head-shake or hand movement) since they won't be able to safeword.

8. Punishments

Being told you'll be 'punished' is often erotic for someone with submissive tendencies. Humiliating punishments could include things like being made to confess every detail of a misdemeanour, beg for forgiveness or perform some kind of task. Or you could discipline them physically, which we'll talk about later in this chapter.

9. Forced orgasm

Inflicting orgasms on your partner can be lots of fun – and best of all, it's you who gets to decide how they get to come and how many times! A Hitachi Magic Wand is the ultimate tool for forcing a woman to orgasm. For men, try some of the electro play toys like rubber cock loops. Alternatively, if he's into anal play, stimulate him anally while you order him to masturbate.

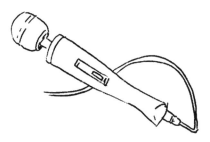

Hitachi Magic Wand

10. Tease and denial

Get your lover to perform all sorts of sex acts, but make it clear they must beg for permission to come. When they do, deny them. Do this over and over again for maximum frustration.

You can combine this with ordering them to make you come over and over without granting them release. You're the one in charge, so whether you let them climax at the end of the scene is, of course, your choice!

If you want to take things further, ban your lover from orgasming for several days before the scene. Make it difficult for them by demanding they masturbate or have sex with you without climaxing. As the tension builds, they'll find themselves in a perpetual state of arousal. When you eventually allow them to come, it'll be intense.

A word of warning: being in such a perpetual state of excitement can make it hard to concentrate on anything, including work! So you might want to save this one for a holiday or the weekend.

'Orgasm control' is a variation on this where you combine some of these techniques with trigger words and actions, like counting down to climax, as you can see here.

> **Orgasm Control**
>
> Just as I'm about to come, he stops. "Don't you dare come." he says in that low, firm voice that I know means business. "Don't you dare come without Master's permission, Slut."

"Please Master, may I come?" I beg.

"No. You will come when Master tells you to come."

Those words turn me on more than anything else he could say or do. I am filled with gratitude for his control over me, much more gratitude than I could ever have for him granting me release.

I know I am not to come without permission. If I do there will be punishments. But my Master is kind and I am grateful when he disciplines me. What I dread is his disapproval. I love more than anything to make him proud by obeying his every instruction perfectly, pleasing and serving him in the way he wants and commands.

He begins fingering me again – he knows just how to drive me wild. And when I'm right on the edge, I beg him frantically, "Please Master, may I come? Please!" He leans close to my ear and in a low, firm voice he says, "No, you may not. Master controls when you orgasm."

Then he draws away, looks me in the eye and delivers a sharp, controlled slap to my cheek. Not hard, but it shocks me. I'm gasping with surprise and absolutely soaking wet. Seeing how turned on his slap makes me, he shoots me a sadistic little smile.

I feel another rush of gratitude flood through me. It is so strong it feels like an emotional orgasm. I am used to controlling everything in life, but that's not how it works with him. When we're in scene, I am entirely under his spell. He knows exactly how giving up power turns me on, and I know he loves taking power just as much. We are two sides of the same coin.

Now he is playing with me again. "Master, please may I come!" I call out, all self-respect and dignity entirely gone.

"Look me in the eye," he orders. "You will look Master in the eye and you will come when I reach zero."

I meet his eye and he starts counting. "Ten, nine, eight, seven..."

I am writhing, desperate to come but even more desperate to obey him, to make him proud of me.

"...six, five, four..."

I'm moaning, deep in his eyes, just about holding off – and it's taking such self-control. But every fibre of my being wants to serve him perfectly and please him by coming on cue.

"...three..." he pauses. Yes, he does – oh my God, he pauses!

"...two... one... Come for me Slut!"

And I come, powerfully, convulsing, crying out, for what seems like forever, all the time meeting his gaze as he demands, knowing I have served him well, that I have pleased him and made him proud.

As my orgasm fades, he holds me close. "Such a good girl," he says gently, kissing me and stroking my hair. "Master is so proud of his slut. Such a good, obedient slut."

I feel a rush of pleasure and pride. This man cares deeply about what I need, and he loves giving it to me.

> I feel so safe lying here with him. So respected, so cherished, so loved.

PLEASURE/PAIN PLAY

Ever enjoyed someone pinching your nipple, hard? Scratching your back? Or even biting? All sorts of sensations can be fun when you're sexually aroused. In the heat of the moment it feels passionate and arousing, but if they walked up to you while you were watching TV and pinched you it wouldn't feel so great!

With a warm-up, with the right intensity and with a lover who knows what they're doing, pleasure/pain play can give you an incredible rush of sexual pleasure. It's like eating spicy food: you wouldn't bite into a raw chilli, but a little of it in a hot curry gives you quite a kick.

Pain play releases your endorphins, the body's pain killing chemicals, which gives you the most incredible high you can imagine. But to experience that requires a careful build-up, beginning perhaps with light spanks, then stronger ones, and then perhaps a paddle. More and more endorphins are released at each level so the sensation literally *does not feel like pain, but pleasure.* A sudden onset of pain, like the one you get when you stub your toe, feels completely different, as there hasn't been that gradual build-up of endorphins to give you a rush.

SAFETY FIRST!

When using striking toys, concentrate on the areas of the body that are well-padded. In particular, do not use them on the stomach, kidneys, lower back, ankles, toes, fingers, joints, face, neck or the tops of the feet. Safer areas include the buttocks, thighs, upper back and even the soles of the feet. With caution, you can also lightly strike the breasts, chest area and female genitals.

Where do I start with pleasure/pain play?

Work up to the scene by using some of the anticipation, lead-up or role play techniques described earlier in this book.

- Go slowly, build up gradually, pay close attention to the way your partner responds and if in doubt, ask for feedback. You'll soon learn to read your partner and know when to go harder or softer.

- You're responsible for your lover's physical and emotional safety when they're tied up and vulnerable, so use common sense. Don't use toys on your lover if you haven't checked how they feel on yourself, and never leave them tied up unattended.

- Start with simple things: pinching, biting, spanking or scratching. You can combine this with bondage or role play if you like.

- Experiment with lightly slapping the genital area – you might be surprised how good this feels.

Pain is just another type of sensation so check out the Sensation Play chapter for ideas, too. You can take things like wax, nipple clamps and electro play up a notch or two, slowly building the sensation as you would for spanking or paddling.

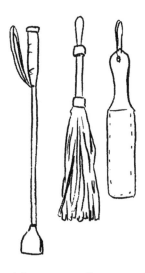

from left to right: a crop, flogger and paddle

PADDLING

If you enjoy being spanked, you'll probably like being paddled, too. Using a paddle saves the spanker's hand from getting sore so they have more stamina.

If you're buying a paddle, invest in a larger one to start with – it may look intimidating but the sensation it gives is far milder than a small one as the force is spread over a larger area. Paddles made of hard materials like wood tend to feel more intense than those made of flexible things like leather. You could also opt for a paddle with fur on one side, which feels fantastic trailed over the skin between strikes.

Start with light, fast strokes, focusing on the sweet spot (see The Art of Spanking section in Chapter 7) and build up your intensity gradually, always staying alert to your lover's reactions so you don't hurt them, but instead get those endorphins pumping to bring that intoxicating rush.

A man should never hit a woman – or should he?

There are plenty of feminist writers who defend a woman's right to choose to have rough sex. What you do in bed doesn't have widespread international ramifications; politics and sex are separate. Some people – men as well as women – just find it fun to surrender, whether that's through pain play or just taking orders. As long as both of you consent, just have fun with it and don't worry what others might think. It's none of their business.

CROPPING

Crops are sharp, precise and give a lovely stinging sensation that's unlike anything else. The psychological association with equestrianism is also hot, and they can be great for headmaster/student role plays or even interrogation scenes.

Beware of novelty crops; to create the needed sensation you'll need a well-made implement without loose or frayed edges. If you're new to using a crop, start by striking the buttocks, as there's plenty of cushioning there. Make sure the end of the crop strikes flat against your lover's skin. Just a light flick of the wrist gives quite a strong sensation.

As usual you'll need to warm up, so a light spanking is perfect. Tap the crop lightly and quickly before increasing the intensity. As always, stay in tune with your lover so you know how far and fast to go.

As you become more confident you can move on to crop other parts of your lover's body. Light crops across the inner thighs, breasts and nipples feel divine, and if your partner is keen you can try lightly cropping the genitals. Be careful with these areas and as usual, start lightly and work your way up.

You can increase the intensity with flogging or caning, but these require advanced techniques that are beyond the scope of this book. (Check out thekinkysexbook.com for more information.)

TAKING THINGS FURTHER

We're used to feeling spurred on by a challenge when it comes to our working lives. Most (though not all) of us find a repetitive job boring; we crave progress, the chance to learn and do something that stretches us. It's the same with sex – doing the same thing every time just gets dull. But if you're with someone who challenges your boundaries and tests your limits in a safe, consensual way, things get a lot more interesting. But to do that you both need to clearly articulate your limits.

HARD AND SOFT LIMITS

Hard limits are things that you absolutely will not do, under any circumstances, and they are always to be respected. But there are also soft limits – things that you usually won't do, but under certain circumstances and with the right person, you might.

Self-exploration is about going beyond your known world; you can't know your limits if you've never tested them. When someone pushes your soft limits, they take you just slightly outside of your comfort zone so you can see how it feels. You're trusting them to look after you when you're in uncharted territory, which forms a profound bond. If you've been together with your lover for some time, this can add another layer of depth to your relationships.

I've personally experienced situations when my lover suggested something that didn't particularly appeal at first, but when we acted it out I found it incredibly sexy. So I adopted a new policy: within limits, try everything once, even if at first it doesn't appeal. I never looked back.

Exploring your boundaries helps you get to know yourself and your partner in a deeper way than ever before, if you're open to experimenting. Consider this kind of scenario.

Tied

He knows just how to tie me. Gently, almost affectionately, he ties my wrists so I can't wriggle out, yet the knot does not tighten when I struggle. He ties my hands and ankles to the bedposts so I am spread eagle for him, fully clothed and blindfolded. I am breathing hard. I don't know what to expect.

He moves away and all I can do is wait there for him, panting in anticipation, wondering what he'll do next. He loves to see me like this, wanting him so much yet unable to have him. He loves to tease me.

He takes the blindfold off and I see he has a knife. I gasp. I knew we would do this but somehow it's still a shock.

He puts the cool flatness of the blade against my chest, looking into my eyes. "Don't move," he says. "You trust Master, don't you?"

"Yes," I whisper.

He positions the blade just under the skirt of my dress and starts to cut upwards, stripping it away from my skin. He cuts slowly, savouring my trembling breathlessness. I hear the sound of the fabric being sliced from my body.

I am lying there tied to the bed, on display for him. Then with two quick cuts, my bra is gone.

I feel so vulnerable as he gently trails the tip of the knife slowly across my breasts. I am breathing hard but he is careful, oh so careful, not to cut me. He pinches my nipple and kisses my mouth hard, demandingly. His kiss says, "I am going to have you and you are helpless to resist." Then slowly, nonchalantly, he trails the tip of the knife down my bare skin to my panties. I am shaking uncontrollably with dread and desire.

"Stay very still," he commands. I hold my breath and obey, watching him.

He slides the blade slowly under the gusset of my panties and skin... oh God it feels so smooth and cold against my pussy! Then he tilts the knife up, slicing through the fabric of my knickers. Finding them totally drenched, he looks pleased. Finally I release my breath. I lie there, panting, tied, naked and totally exposed for him, his to do with whatever he wants.

He trails his fingers slowly over my breasts, enjoying the way my body reacts. He pushes two fingers inside my dripping wet cunt and I gasp in surprise.

"Poor Slut, so helpless for Master," he says sadistically. "Struggle for me, let's see if you can escape."

I struggle but it's no use. He pulls his fingers out, relishing the power he has over me, and brings his face close to mine.

"Master owns his slut, doesn't he?" he says holding eye contact.

"Yes!" I gasp passionately, in that moment completely his.

"Say it."

"Master, you own me!"

"You're Master's three-holed fuck-toy, aren't you?"

"Yes, Master!"

I am writhing at his words, longing for him to touch me.

"Say it. Keep saying it."

"I am Master's three-holed fuck toy! I am Master's three-holed fuck-toy! I am Master's three-holed fuck-toy!"

As I repeat, he reaches down and brushes against my pussy. So lightly, so teasingly.

"Mmmm, your cunt is so wet. Would Slut like Master's cock in it?"

"Oh yes please Master!"

"Beg me."

"Master please fuck me! Please!"

He looks into my eyes as he pushes against my lips, teasing my pussy with his cock.

"You want it, don't you?"

"Yes Master!"

"Who owns you?"

"You own me Master!"

And with those words he thrusts into me, filling me up entirely as I writhe about, tied and helpless. A ridiculous thought flits across my mind: this is the missionary position – all hail the plain old, ordinary missionary position! I stifle a giggle and this earns me a slap across my cheek. I look at him in shame and glory.

He slows his pace. He never, ever comes without controlling it.

He's fucking me hard. "Now come for Master like a good, obedient slut," he orders. And holding his gaze I come instantly, crying out as waves of pleasure wash through me.

He grips my hair and says, "I own you."

"Yes, you own me," I say.

"Repeat it."

"You own me Master! You own me Master! You own me Master!"

And seconds later, he is coming, too – loudly, possessively, thrusting into me as he looks into my eyes.

CHAPTER 10
·····················

BONDAGE FOR BEGINNERS

Bondage, it seems, is the bees' knees. Sex toy shops are doing a roaring trade in cuffs, straps and rope kits and a recent survey by Yahoo! found 62% of women said they'd either tied someone up or been tied up during sex. So what's so exciting about being restrained?

We're used to being in control of our bodies so having our movement restricted is an unusual experience. It concentrates your mind in a unique way, intensely sensitising your skin to your lover's touch. And it can even reverse the power balance: suddenly the stronger partner, who could usually wriggle free, becomes quite helpless.

Bondage is often central to role play – what fun is a prisoner or kidnap scenario without restraints for you to struggle against? And if you're the one tying, there's the heady thrill of gift-wrapping your lover as if for your own pleasure and a deepening of trust as they give themselves to you in such an intimate, all-or-nothing way. What's seldom understood by those who haven't been tied up is that even on an emotional level, bondage is bonding.

That's because it requires more trust than almost any other activity – this is not something you want to be doing on a one-night stand! It's also something that requires a little skill and knowledge if you're to play safely. In this chapter you'll discover:

- How to safely tie your lover up – no knots necessary
- How to create your own bondage bed in minutes
- Four favourite bondage positions
- What to do with your lover once you have them tied
- Rope-free ways to restrain your lover

I'm a highly driven person and most of the time my life feels like I'm just about holding it all together, but when I'm tied up the pressure of my day-to-day responsibilities falls away and I'm entirely in that moment. I can't **do** *anything, which means I can't do anything* **wrong**. *For a while I can let those balls I'm juggling fall, surrendering myself to the sensations and the deepening connection with my lover. It's like letting someone take the wheel when you're exhausted from driving. For a control freak like me it's the ultimate release.* – **Felicity**

HOW DO I BRING THIS UP WITH MY LOVER?

Many people are curious about trying bondage but hold back because they just don't know where to begin, so there's every chance your lover could have thought about it already. Here are some ways to break the ice.

Ban the 'B' word: Some people associate the word 'bondage' with things like horror movies or slavery. You might find it's less confronting to say something like "I'd love to tie you to the bed and tease you."

Take the pressure off: Telling your lover you've wanted to do this your whole life could well scare them off. Instead, talk about it as a one-off experience for you to try together. Point out that they'll get to be pleasured without having to do a thing.

Show and tell: If you like the idea of being tied down, ask your lover to pin you to the bed in the heat of the moment. Let them see how turned on it makes you and throw out a little comment like, "It really turns me on when you're in control." If your tastes run in the opposite direction, try pinning your lover to the bed and saying, "You're so hot when you're at my mercy like this." Then, watch their response. If they seem to like it, have a chat about it afterwards and suggest you push things further next time.

SAFETY FIRST!

Avoid tying someone tightly or leaving them in the same position for too long. Cutting off circulation will give them pins and needles, which is distinctly unsexy.

Check in regularly for any signs of tingling or numbness and release your lover immediately if they occur.

Always have a pair of scissors to hand. Bandage scissors (also called EMT scissors) are ideal. They're designed to be slipped under a bandage so it can be cut without injuring the person, so they have one sharp blade and one with a rounded tip. They're inexpensive and you can buy them from most pharmacies.

Don't leave rope marks. Many people dread the idea of explaining marks or bruises to family, friends and colleagues, but if you tie carefully or use cuffs, you won't leave any trace. The key is to spread the tension across a wider section of skin so it doesn't cut in if your lover struggles. Any redness or rope impressions usually disappear by the next day.

Avoid knots that tighten when pulled, and opt for those with a quick release.

Don't gag your partner. Being both bound and gagged the first time you try bondage is too much too soon, and it's likely to put them off. On top of that, to make the experience pleasurable you'll need to hear their feedback about what it feels like to be touched, licked, nibbled, pinched or otherwise stimulated. Once you're comfortable taking things further and if both of you are keen, it's fine to use a gag. However, you may not hear your lover's safeword, so it's best to agree beforehand on a signal to use (perhaps a shake of the head or a hand gesture).

WHERE DO I START?

Play safe. Bondage requires a lot of trust, so it's important to know exactly what you're doing before you even bring up the idea. If you read and follow the safety tips in this chapter you'll be able to confidently reassure your lover you've researched this and know exactly what you're doing.

Talk about it beforehand. As with all aspects of kinky sex, talking or 'negotiating' beforehand is vital since it will reveal your lover's fantasies, hard and soft limits. Being completely bound for the first time can be intimidating, so find out if they'd prefer you to bind only their wrists for now.

Take things slowly. Many people associate rope with kidnapping or torture, so for the first time it could be better to use men's ties or a soft dressing gown belt. You'll look spontaneous, which eases the pressure: you haven't just gone out and bought a full bondage kit, gimp mask and flogger! Avoid using stockings or silk scarfs, as they tend to bunch up painfully and can be hard to untie.

Which rope is best for bondage?

Normal nylon rope that you can buy from DIY stores is inexpensive, soft and readily available. Cotton rope is extremely gentle on the skin. Jute and hemp is the crème de la crème: popular for Japanese rope bondage, it's made from natural fibres and is slightly rough, which means it feels incredible trailed sensually across the skin. Thicker rope provides more surface area and therefore less strain, so choose rope that's 6mm to 8mm (one-quarter to one-third of an inch) in diameter in a selection of 5-metre and 10-metre lengths.

Make them the star of the show and do everything possible to please them. They might feel silly, so reassure them by telling them how sexy they look tied up and how turned on you are by the way they move against the restraints. Ask for feedback, do the things you know turn them on – and climax only if they do. The idea is to give them such a great time that they'll be begging *you* to do it again!

Keep it sensual. The first time they're tied isn't the time to launch at them with a crop or flogger – unless that's what they like and you've talked about it beforehand. Instead, keep things slow and sensual with a bit of sensation play, perhaps using a tickler or feather duster across their erogenous zones or kissing, licking, nibbling and teasing them.

Ask how they found it afterwards. Give them plenty of affection, tell them how sexy it was for you, and ask them how they felt about the experience. Check in the next day, too, when they'll have had more time to process things. Ask them what they liked and, if appropriate, how you could make it even hotter for them next time.

> I was spanked enough as a kid so that's never appealed to me, but I wasn't tied up so that's always seemed kind of hot. My day job is pretty stressful and sometimes it's so good not to be the one in charge. Being bound lets me give up control – when my boyfriend ties me up I can totally let go. – **John**

HOW TO TIE YOUR LOVER WITHOUT KNOWING FANCY KNOTS

If you're new to bondage and want an easy solution that doesn't involve learning elaborate knots, then wrist and ankle cuffs are your friends. They're comfortable, fast to take on and off, and save you from needing to learn complicated knots. Invest in high-quality, comfortable, buckle-up cuffs (the wider ones are more comfortable), not the Velcro kind, as they're easier to work yourself free from.

Two lengths of rope, two ankle cuffs and two wrist cuffs are all you really need to do most rope bondage for restraint. Snap hooks are optional but very handy. They make it quick and easy to hook a pair of cuffs to eyebolts, rope or pretty much anything – perfect if you'd rather not fiddle with fancy knots in the heat of the moment. You can restrain your partner in just a second, and free them just as fast.

Beware of cheap ankle and wrist cuffs – they can chafe, irritate and even leave marks. To find high quality, comfortable cuffs at very reasonable prices, go to my free 'Secret Sex Toy Guide' at http://thekinkysexbook.com/secret-sex-toys/.

> *The sight of a tightly bound man who's helplessly restrained is so sexy. I get really excited when I see him struggle against the ropes. I hear him breathing heavily, see the sweat on his forehead, his muscles tense as they strain against the rope. It's such fun to turn the tables.*
>
> **– Emily**

CREATE YOUR OWN BONDAGE BED IN MINUTES

Damn, I hear you say – my bed doesn't have any anchor points! Fortunately, these simple solutions allow you to tie your lover to any bed quickly and easily, even if you know nothing about knots.

Here's a fast, inexpensive option that works with pretty much all beds. You'll need just two long pieces of rope, two wrist cuffs and two ankle cuffs, all with metal D-rings.

- Slip one long piece of rope through the D-rings on the wrist cuffs, and lie the rope across the head of the bed so one end touches the floor.

- Slide the cuffs along the rope until you have them where you'd like them to be, and tie them in place. You'll now have one piece of rope across the mattress with two wrist cuffs tied to it.

- Slip the long end of the rope underneath the mattress, bring it back up the other side, and tie the two ends of the rope together with a couple of granny knots. You'll now have a length of rope looped all the way around the mattress, with two wrist cuffs tied to it.

- Do the same thing with the other length of rope and the ankle cuffs at the foot of the bed. You now have an easy way to restrain your lover spread eagle to the bed.

Use a variation on this idea to tie your lover to pretty much anything: a chair, kitchen table, coffee table, banisters – even your white picket fence!

OFF-THE-SHELF BONDAGE KITS

DIY bondage not your thing? Ready-made, inexpensive under-the-mattress bondage kits are ideal for beginners and can easily be ordered online. They have nylon straps that connect under the mattress and come with four Velcro or buckle-up cuffs. It's less versatile than using your own rope, but there's still a whole lot of fun to be had and they're lightweight, portable and simple to use.

If you want to restrict their movement. Tie various bits of their body together, perhaps binding their wrists in front or behind them or their ankles or knees together. Even just tying your lover's wrists together can have a profound psychological effect. From this position you can order them to kneel, feed them, or demand they perform oral sex on you.

Under-bed Bondage Kit

If you want to use toys on them, provoke a feeling of vulnerability or tie them during sex. Bind them so their limbs are spread apart. Open leg ties will make them feel especially exposed and available.

If you're tying them as part of a role play. Cable ties are ideal for binding wrists and ankles together. They're fast and easy to use and there is absolutely no way to wriggle out of them! Make sure you buy the wider, 10mm kind, which are used by the police riot force, as the traditional thinner ones will cut into the skin.

Cable ties

FOUR FAVOURITE BONDAGE POSITIONS

It's time to get creative. Look around your home – what could you do with each piece of furniture? When you think of being tied up, you probably imagine being bound spread-eagle to a bed, but there are so many other options. Here are my favourite four.

Bound to a chair

It's easy to tie your lover to a chair using wrist and ankle cuffs. Put their arms behind the back of the chair and either slip the rope through the D-rings of the cuffs to tie their wrists together, or use a snap hook to fasten their wrists. Attach thigh cuffs to a length of rope passed under the chair to spread their legs. Thread the rope through the D-rings of the thigh cuffs and wind it round each chair leg to hold them firmly in place.

Legs up

This is the same as spanking position number 4 in Chapter 7, The Science of Spanking, and it offers so many possibilities for play. It works best if the person bound wears thigh cuffs, but ankle cuffs will work too. Your lover lies on their back at the edge of the bed, knees lifted and legs spread. Fasten the rope at the bed legs above their head, then attach it to their thigh or ankle cuffs and shorten the rope until their legs are up in the air. It's a very vulnerable feeling to be bound with your knees bent and legs spread wide, and the psychological impact can be blissfully intense.

Standing

This give you access to both sides of your lover's body and allow you to easily change their position, so you can perhaps spank them bent over and then turn them round for some sensation play on their nipples. A spreader bar is ideal for this position: it's a rigid metal bar with cuffs at each end that prevents your partner from closing their legs. The best ones can be adjusted so you can spread their legs as wide as you like.

Spreader Bar

Hogtied

This position restrains your lover's wrists and ankles behind their back. An adjustable hogtie kit makes this quick and easy – it comes with four snap hooks that you can attach to the D-rings of your own wrist and ankle cuffs, restraining your partner either on their side or tummy.

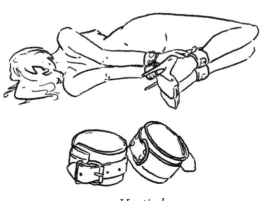

Hogtied

Not sure what you could do in that position? Here's a story that might inspire you.

Hogtied

I'm hogtied on the bed, wrists and ankles bound, on my stomach for my Master's viewing pleasure. He's positioned me between his legs as he reclines against the headboard. I'm propped up with pillows so my mouth is level with his perfect cock. Oh, how I want it in my mouth. I look at it longingly but he's sure to keep it just out of reach.

"Mmmm, Slut looks so helpless," he says, surveying me in my glorious submission. How is it, I think, that when I'm like this for him I feel more in my power than ever?

"Struggle for Master," he says, fixing me with his dominant gaze.

I obey.

"Aw, poor Slut. You can't get away, can you?"

I struggle more and shake my head. He has taken away my permission to speak.

Sometimes when I'm like this he asks me questions to trick me into talking. He knows if I speak it's an excuse to punish me. And he loves punishing me, almost as much as I love taking his punishments.

"Such a good, obedient Slut. You want Master's cock in your mouth, don't you?"

I nod passionately.

"Well you can't have it. Not yet. Master has plans for you first."

I'm wondering what he will do to me. My heart races with excitement.

He sits up, leans over and takes out a big, shiny metal hook with a ball on one end and a ring on the other. I gasp. He's shown me one of these before online and asked if I would like him to use me with it. He saw how much the idea turned me on. How thoughtful he is.

He ties some rope to the ring end of the hook and puts the ball end against my pussy. I shudder – it's so cold.

"Now this will hurt a little," he says, pushing it in gently. I am writhing. It feels so cold. I feel so humiliated.

"Good girl," he says once it's all the way in. "Such a good, obedient girl for Master." I nod again. I love it when he's proud of me.

He lies back against the headboard again, looking at me as I lie there on my stomach with my head between his legs, bound hand and foot with the hook inside me and the rope draped over my body. Offhandedly, he pulls on the rope, and as it tightens, the ball end of the hook within me moves. Wow! What a sensation! I am gasping with desire.

His cock is still centimetres from my mouth, teasing me. I'm staring at it, aching to have him in my mouth, to please and delight him, to have him use me, to fuck my mouth.

"I think Slut wants to show Master what a cock-slut she is. Hmmm?"

I nod eagerly and he pushes his cock oh-so-slowly into my waiting mouth. With one hand, he softly grips my hair and slowly fucks my mouth, watching my face closely so he goes nice and deep but is careful not to make me gag. At the same time, looking into my eyes, he pulls on the rope and the hook moves inside me.

As he slowly thrusts into me he speaks gently, almost tenderly.

"Mmmm, so warm and wet. Just like a cunt."

He sees how I writhe and moan at these words.

"That's what your mouth is to me, isn't it? Just a cunt for me to fuck."

At these words I'm almost coming.

"You're my three-holed fuck-toy, aren't you? So good at serving Master. Such a good girl. Mmmm, Master likes fucking his slut's cunt-mouth."

I feel delightfully degraded and used, having my mouth fucked while he pulls the hook in my pussy. I'm writhing and moaning and I can hear his breathing getting faster. He's loving having me like this for him.

"Slut's enjoying serving Master, aren't you?"

I nod eagerly. He's still leaning back on the bed, looking deeply into my eyes. I know he realises I'm on the point of orgasm.

"Look at me. That's right. Now, make Master proud. Come for Master like a good girl. Come!" he orders me.

And as he pulls on the hook in my pussy I climax violently, quietly convulsing as my moans of pleasure are muffled, gagged by his cock, which is still buried deep in my mouth.

WHAT TO DO WHEN YOU HAVE YOUR LOVER TIED UP

As you can see, tying someone up is where the fun starts. There are so many things you can do once you have your lover bound.

'Tie and tease' can be a wonderful turn-on: it's hot to be taken to the brink time and time again. When you do get to come, your orgasm will be super-intense.

Bondage can also be used to train your lover – you'll find them a very willing pupil when they know they'll be rewarded for good performance with an orgasm! Give a close-up demonstration of where you touch yourself and how, show them how you like toys used on you or talk them through every lick and suck as they perform oral sex on you, describing each sensation as you order them to bring you to climax.

If you want to explore sensation (and who doesn't?) you'll find plenty of ideas in Sensation Play (Chapter 6). And if you're keen on pleasure/pain play, take the opportunity to administer a little punishment with a paddle, crop, cane or even an electro-insertable.

ROPE FOR SENSUAL RESTRAINT

There's more to bondage than tying someone up and having sex with them – in fact, the act of tying and untying can be incredibly sensual. Caress your lover with the rope, drawing it across erogenous zones and sensitive areas. Use it to pinch a nipple or slowly drag it across their neck, gently tightening it before releasing.

Many people love having their hair pulled so if your partner has long hair, tying their hair can be a huge turn-on. Try trailing the rope between your lover's legs, drawing it up between her labia or tightening it around his cock. Rope transmits vibration well, so for even more fun, take a vibrator to the rope and watch as your lover squirms helplessly in delight.

JAPANESE ROPE BONDAGE

At the pinnacle of rope bondage technique lies the visually stunning Japanese rope bondage, Shibari, also known as Kinbaku. It's as much an art form as a bondage technique, the tying and untying similar to performance art or simply the act of creating a beautiful but transient living sculpture. What emerges is a series of aesthetically striking but functional geometric patterns that hold you, perhaps even suspending you entirely.

Many people find that when they're bound, they fall into the trance-like state of 'rope space', a dreamy, relaxed, euphoric state similar to subspace. I've experienced it when bound in Shibari, and for me it feels as though every muscle in my body can relax, since the rope is holding me together, like an all-over embrace. Flooded with endorphins, my muscles relax, my speech slurs and it feels like I'm floating.

Shibari takes a long time to learn but it's worth it if you're a bondage enthusiast, as the sensations and aesthetic are incomparable. If you're interested in learning, search the internet for local classes in your area.

Think bondage is all about rope? Think again! There are many sexy, sensual ways to restrain your lover I bet you haven't thought of. Here are just two of them.

VETRAP

This is one of my favourite bondage toys – the feel of it when you're bound is unlike anything else, yet it's so little known!

Vetrap (pronounced Vet-rap) is stretchy, self-adhesive bandaging tape used for binding animals' limbs. You can use it to totally immobilise someone, but unlike Saran Wrap it's sold in 10cm-wide rolls so it's easy to bind just one part of them. Having your arms bound behind your back with Vetrap feels amazing – it stretches a little when you struggle against it, which gives you a safe, cosy feeling while still being totally at your lover's mercy.

If you bend a limb and bind it, your lover won't be able to extend it. Binding every limb like this brings a whole lot of opportunities, whether you put them on their back and play with them or hoist them face-down onto their elbows and knees.

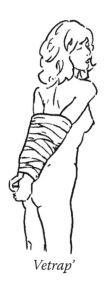

Vetrap'

Vetrap is inexpensive and comes in a range of colours – it's great fun in the festive season to wrap your lover up like a Christmas present in red, yellow and green! Although you can buy it from pet stores, it's cheapest on eBay.

SARAN WRAP

Known less glamorously in hardware stores as 'pallet wrap', Saran Wrap comes in 50mm (20 inch) wide rolls and looks similar to heavy-duty cling wrap. It's fast and easy to wrap someone in, feels snug and sexy, and offers a world of sensation play opportunities.

To use it, order your lover to stand with their hands by their sides as you wrap them from shoulders to feet, tightly cocooning them in an all-over body restraint. They may be unstable on their feet, so to prevent them falling over, lie them down after they're wrapped. Rip holes in strategic places and stimulate any part of your lover's body without ropes getting in the way.

It's easy to overheat when you're wrapped up so check on your lover regularly, and if they're wrapped for any length of time give them water to prevent dehydration. When you're done, just rip it off their body. They'll cool down fast, so have blankets or a warm bath robe to hand.

The best place to buy Saran Wrap inexpensively is – you've guessed it – your trusty local hardware store. Just ask for a roll of pallet wrap and tell them which colour you'd prefer. Some people find it a turn-on to see their lover wrapped in the transparent stuff, but black is the favourite.

Wrapping your partner up for bondage brings many new play opportunities. Since they're bound to themselves, rather than tied down to anything, it's easy to move them into different positions. If you're feeling really evil, put a remote control vibrator inside them before you wrap them.

First Time

Pallet wrap – who'd have thought it would feel so good? I'm standing here, tightly wrapped in black, shiny plastic from shoulders to feet, unable to move even a finger. This is the first time he's dominated me. I am totally at his mercy and I'm loving every second.

He looks me in the eye and, with a mildly amused look and the slightest, most casual push, knocks me completely off balance.

Panic floods through me as I fall backwards through the air, totally restrained and helpless to break my fall. I land safely on the bed and I know at this point that I trust him completely. He's planned every single move. I am his toy, his plaything. In this time, I exist solely for his amusement.

I'm ordered to try to free myself, so I wriggle helplessly as his eyes fill with lust. Seeing me so vulnerable is turning him on.

He tears two holes in the wrap for my breasts and pinches my nipples, hard. I gasp. Then he rips another hole for my pussy and touches me gently, teasingly. I hold back – I don't want to come. I don't like to come the first time I'm with someone. I like to stay in control.

I look at him in turmoil, wrestling with my emotions. People do things on my terms. I'm not used to giving up control. This new feeling of letting go is terrifying but so thrilling. As he puts a vibrator against me, I know I am lost.

And I can see in his eyes he knows what I'm thinking. His penetrating look says it all: "You're playing by my rules now, not yours."

"Look at me," he demands. He is getting off on the power he has over me. The power of bringing a strong, assertive woman down, and of watching me love every second of it. I can see it in his eyes. It's a look I've never seen before – so intense, so controlling, so damn hot that I can't stand it anymore.

And at that point I realise with a delicious rush of humiliation that he's going to force me to climax whether I like it or not. Within seconds I come loudly, writhing and bucking, all the time obediently holding his gaze.

CHAPTER 11

ROLE PLAY

Cops and robbers, doctors and nurses – as children we understand how play and imagination enrich our lives. But as we grow up we get sensible, start worrying about paying bills and doing everything we can to be taken seriously at work. Slowly but surely our responsibilities squeeze out the last vestiges of playfulness in us and we begin feeling old. What a drag.

In today's world we're often judged on the car we drive, the job we have and the clothes we wear. It's confining, so being someone else for a while feels amazingly liberating. It's exhilarating to let yourself go and be truly in the moment without any expectations of acceptable behaviour.

If you've never tried it, you might just think the whole thing silly and embarrassing – I know I did at first. But once I gave it a go I realised pretending to be someone else is fun. It stimulates feelings of excitement and attraction because it's new, and the mind finds novelty sexy. You have nothing to lose but your inhibitions.

HOW DO I BRING THIS UP WITH MY LOVER?

Role play is best approached with a sense of playfulness and fun. Keep it light-hearted and start with something easy and appealing to act out.

Read your lover a sexy story or hire a DVD featuring something you'd like to enact. Test the waters by saying something like "I found that spy scene in the movie so sexy. How about we try that out sometime?"

Fancy dress parties are a great excuse to be someone else for a while, and telling your lover how hot they'd look as a cop should get the hint across. Start flirting as though he's arresting you. From there it's a small step to suggesting you enact a scene in costume.

Some people may feel that if you want them to play a role you're really wishing you were with someone else, so reassure your lover this is something you think would be fun for both of you to experiment with as a one-off, and just see how you both find it. Do everything you can to plan an experience that's as thrilling and satisfying for your lover as possible so they'll want to do it again. If you're shy about doing the whole dress-up thing, don't worry – often just one accessory and a good sense of humour is all that's needed.

I love the pure escapism of role play. My girlfriend and I can be anyone we want, which gets rid of any hang-ups and makes us far more free with each other than usual. Acting out a character opens up possibilities I wouldn't usually consider. It's easier to reveal our deepest desires to each other. I find we connect in a completely different way. **– Sarah**

I'm often teased by friends for my love of suits: a powerful looking man in a well-cut pinstripe really does make me weak at the knees, and don't ask me why but somehow the effect is heightened if he's carrying a briefcase! It took only a few jokes about this from my friends for my ex to realise he could use this to his advantage. So one day, he rocked up on my doorstep in his pinstripe suit. Before I knew it, we were flirtatiously planning an office role-play scene. As it turned out, his briefcase was more than a sexy prop — I never realised how many toys it could hold! **– Karen**

Planning a role play is often just as exciting as actually doing it. Getting the right clothes, buying the accessories or talking about what to do all add to the sense of fun, adventure and anticipation and create a kind of naughty, secret world you inhabit together for a while. You're creating something that's uniquely yours, so let go and have a laugh.

WHERE DO I START?

Begin with both of you describing some of your fantasies as outlined in Chapter 4. Have you always dreamt of being spanked as a schoolgirl? Seduced by a hooker? Interrogating someone, complete with a strip-search? You wouldn't do theses things in real life, but playing a role with a loving partner gives you a safe outlet to live out your fantasies.

You'll often find you're more drawn to enacting a particular role in your fantasy. One of you, for example, may be turned on by the idea of being an authority figure, whereas the other might like the idea of being ordered around. Since most role plays rely on uneven power dynamics for their eroticism, partners who enjoy Dominance/submission will find role play adds another dimension.

Planning the room's set-up can help you both get into character. Whether you want a bare light bulb and chair for an interrogation scene or a massage table for a medical one, it all helps create the suspension of belief that allows you to let go and live a different life for a little while.

ROLE PLAYING – A POWER TRIP?

Why are so many of the role plays that turn us on things that in real life would be horribly traumatic or exploitative? Sex therapists believe small doses of negative emotions like anger, guilt, and anxiety actually stimulate arousal, since they get your pulse racing and endorphins flooding your system. These are the exact emotions triggered during role play: you've been caught doing something bad (guilt), you're punishing someone for a misdemeanour (anger), you're nervous about what's coming next (anxiety).

Role play lets you explore the excitement of power dynamics safely without getting hurt, much as you do when you watch a movie with an evil villain in it. Not only is this extremely arousing, it also offers a way for you to release the tension associated with these negative emotions, when they accumulate in daily life. So forget analysing why you like the idea of playing a sadistic interrogator or helpless victim – it's a turn-on and a stress reliever, so just enjoy it!

TOP TEN ROLE PLAYING SCENARIOS

It goes without saying that all of these scenes need to be planned and negotiated together so everyone's limits are respected. The opportunities are endless, but here are a few ideas to get you started.

1. Doctor and patient

Your doctor kindly agrees to a house call and arrives dressed, of course, in a lab coat with a stethoscope and clipboard. After increasingly intrusive questions s/he puts on some latex gloves and closely examines you all over, diligently testing your 'reflexes'. Perhaps Doctor needs to use a flashlight to subject you to an internal exam ("Just lie back and spread your legs nice and wide, so I can get a really good look. If there's anything I can do to help you relax...") If you're the doctor, keep a cool, professional demeanour and if you're the patient, act confused at how turned on you're getting. Medical supplies are easily available from your local pharmacy.

2. Mad Scientist and Victim

The evil mad scientist, dressed in a disposable gown and latex gloves, has kidnapped her helpless victim, stripped and bound her to an examining table. She proceeds to perform all sorts of depraved experiments on her, probing her vagina with cold metal equipment (a vibrator works well for this), testing her reactions with ice or seeing how many times she can be brought to the brink of orgasm without climaxing. She could experiment to see how wide a probe she can take, how her body responds to electricity, or how many times she can be forced to orgasm. The 'victim' pleads to be set free, but the evil scientist's curiosity is insatiable!

3. Dirty cop and suspect

One of you turns up at the door dressed as a sexy police officer, complete with dark aviator sunglasses so you can't see their eyes. Flash your fake badge, come in and arrest your lover for 'indecent exposure', handcuffing them to the bannisters. Take out a fake gun and stroke your lover's body with it, telling them you can make that nasty little conviction disappear if they do exactly as you say. Add a pair of spreader bars and take things from there.

4. Headmaster / headmistress and student

A naughty schoolboy gets caught by his headmistress doing something bad – looking at porn, masturbating or lifting the schoolgirls' skirts – and needs to be disciplined. Perhaps he's stripped and made to stand in the corner, ordered to beg for forgiveness, then scolded and put over his headmistress' knee for a spanking.

5. Interrogation

You know a vital piece of information – say the location of a drug baron – and your interrogator will stop at nothing to get it. You could start with the dominant partner capturing the suspect, tying them to a chair and shining a torch into their eyes. Use a variety of implements to 'torture' the suspect – clothes pins, floggers and electro play equipment work particularly well, especially a neon wand, which sounds and looks much scarier than it feels.

6. Blackmail

One of you has a dark secret: a long time ago, you did something disgraceful and you'll go to extreme measures to keep it quiet. Then one day the doorbell rings and it's someone from your past with pictures that they threaten to take to the press. Desperate to keep things from going public, you bribe the blackmailer with sexual favours in exchange for their silence. The blackmailer can make any sexual demands on you he chooses and you are 'forced' to obey.

7. Cop and hooker

One of you is a hooker who's sick of being booked by cops, so in revenge you lure one back to your home for a 'freebie'. Once he's inside, you spike his drink and he wakes up tied to a chair naked, gagged and blindfolded. As he sits there unable to see, you change into an outfit you know he loves. You then remove the blindfold and slowly strip, teasing your helpless prisoner mercilessly with your body and bringing him to the brink of orgasm over and over in all sorts of ways without letting him come. Order him to perform certain sexual favours for you or to humiliate himself by begging. Only when you're fully satisfied do you grant him sexual release.

8. Burglary

Wear black clothes and black leather gloves for this one. She leaves the door unlocked at a specific time – leave a one-hour time window so there's an element of surprise. You 'break in', overpowering her in her bedroom so she falls onto the bed (landing on a soft surface means no one hurts themselves in the struggle). Tie her wrists with the wide cable ties used by the police (available from hardware stores), blindfold and gag her, then tie her to the bed with rope. Rummage through her drawers, take her costume jewellery and have your wicked way with her. Then leave the room, change your clothes and come back in as her gallant protector and rescuer, taking her in your arms and comforting her in any way she desires.

9. Security guard and trespasser

A night security guard catches you trespassing on private property and takes you back to the office. He handcuffs you and subjects you to a humiliating strip search and cavity search and explains it's company policy to call the police in such instances. Of course, if the trespasser co-operates, you could come to some other arrangement. Grateful for the chance to get off the hook, the trespasser performs a range of sexual favours.

10. Boss and secretary

In real life, we all know it's reckless to mix business and pleasure. But as you can see here, in role play you can break any taboo you wish.

Annual Review

Everyone wants an evil boss like this. Suave and clean-cut in his suit with a perfectly tied Windsor knot, he towers above me, looking down at me as though I'm his minion. He's a control freak, a micro-manager, a power-hungry corporate ladder climber and a total and utter bastard. Ruthless, cold, cruel, and mouth-wateringly sexy.

The cup of tea I made him was cold by the time he arrived. That got him cross. Then I double-booked a meeting. That made him more cross. It wasn't a good start to my annual review.

I'm dressed in a short, tight black skirt, white blouse, stockings and heels. As I turn away to fetch him another cup of tea I lean over low, giving him a good look up my skirt. Yes, this is my little power trip, the only way I can get my own back. I'm not wearing panties under my nylons and I can feel his eyes on me. I take my time, pretending to be unaware of his gaze.

"You could go far in this job," he comments breezily as I bring him his tea.

"I need someone to take with me on business trips. Someone who'll be on hand for me constantly, someone who'll satisfy my every... desire," he says suggestively, trailing his eyes brazenly across my body.

"There could even be a pay rise for you. Would you like that? Hmmm?"

"Yes Boss," I reply.

"How much do you want a pay rise?"

"Very much."

"Yes, but how much?"

"Well, I'd do pretty much anything for a good pay rise."

"Prove it," he demands.

I'm confused. "What?"

"Words, words, words. If you'd been in business as long as I have you'd know it's actions that count. So I want you to prove how much you want that pay rise."

And that's when he reaches under the desk and brings out a wooden cane. I can't quite believe it.

Standing, he begins slapping the cane into his hand. His eyes are filled with primal lust. I look at him in shock, speechless.

Towering above me, he commands me in a low, firm voice that's impossible to refuse.

"Bend over and put your arms on the desk."

There is no room for argument. I comply obediently, confused at my mounting desire.

"Let's see just how much of a pay rise you want, hmmm? You'll get $5,000 for each strike."

"But..."

"Shut up and take it!" he snaps. "You want that pay rise, don't you?"

"Yes Boss."

I feel humiliated, bent over like this for him. I know he can see right up my skirt, through my stockings to my bare pussy.

"Spread your legs. That's right, nice and wide — I want a really good look," he commands.

"Yes Boss," I say feeling strangely aroused.

"What's your salary now?"

"$50,000 a year, Boss."

Just as I finish saying this he strikes me with the cane. I gasp.

"How much is it now?"

"$55,000 a year," I pant, shocked as the biting sensation of the cane hits my skin.

Again he strikes my arse.

"$60,000!" I call out.

He strikes me three times in quick succession.

"$75,000 a year, Boss!"

It hurts and I feel degraded but my pussy is drenching my stockings. He spreads my cheeks and surveys me, moaning as he takes his time to admire my glistening cunt, then rips my tights to expose me completely. Holding my cheeks apart he runs a finger across my wet pussy lips, amusing himself.

"Hmmm," he says approvingly, his face tantalisingly close. His warm breath on my pussy lips makes me shiver as he closely examines me. My cheeks flush.

"Yes," he says languidly, "I think you just might have what it takes."

He pulls away and canes me again. The sound shatters the silence.

"$80,000!" I cry out.

"I think I want you to call me Master. Would you like to do that?"

"Yes Master," I pant.

Another strike.

"$85,000 Master!"

"Do you want me to stop? We can stop right there at $85,000."

"No!"

The cane comes down again, two more times, stinging my skin. My arse cheeks must be so flushed.

"$95,000 Master!"

"You're a greedy girl, aren't you? You want more don't you?"

Another strike – this one really hard. I am panting, barely able to speak.

"$100,000!"

"Is that enough or are you even more greedy?"

"That's enough, Master!"

"Good Girl," he says as I stand, pulling my skirt down in shame over my burning buttocks. He half-smiles as he watches me, then walks to his desk to sit down, knees wide, unzipping his pinstriped trousers.

"Now be good and come and suck your Master's cock." he commands.

As I kneel he grabs me gently by the hair. He looks into my eyes and forces his cock deep into my wet and waiting mouth. I moan in ecstasy as he pushes deeper into me, fucking my mouth slowly, totally controlled.

"This will be in your new job description. Whenever I command, you're to get on your knees, open those gorgeous lips of yours and let me fuck your mouth. Understand?"

I moan and try to nod, still sucking him. I can't get enough of his gorgeous cock.

"You're to service me with your mouth whenever and wherever I see fit. And if I want to fuck you, you're to bend over obediently, spread your legs, pull your arse cheeks apart, and thank me for using and pleasuring myself with your cunt. Understand?"

I am getting more and more aroused. I nod again, still obediently taking him as he fucks my mouth slowly.

"I will take you however and whenever I want. Your function is simply to give me pleasure. If it gives me pleasure to deny you orgasm, I will deny you. If I feel like seeing you come for my own entertainment, I'll let you come."

He pulls out of my mouth and looks me in the eye with a cruel, hard stare.

"Am I making myself clear?"

> I am not fast enough to reply and this earns me a firm slap across my cheek. I look at him in shock, which quickly dissolves into unbridled desire. I am so wet.
>
> "Yes Master!" I gasp.
>
> And so begins a wonderful working relationship. I've never looked back.

As you can see, role play can add incredible depth to your sex life. There's no reason to do everything at once however; start slowly and work up to more and more adventurous scenarios. And be prepared for surprises, too. Scenarios that don't initially appeal can be unexpectedly huge turn-ons if you're open-minded enough to give them a chance.

The examples here are just a starting point. Get ideas from films, books or real-life situations you find yourself in or hear about. You can also read erotica that centres around the kind of fantasies you want to role play. Let your erotic imagination run wild!

CHAPTER 12

LADIES FIRST: FEMDOM

Ever fantasised about your man focusing all his attention on making you happy, worshipping and serving you in any way you wish? Imagine if he could get just as much pleasure out of pleasing you as you get from having your desires fulfilled – perhaps more. That's what female domination (Femdom) is all about; you're the sexy, confident woman of his dreams, and he'll love the feeling of giving up control to you.

I believe more women should try this kind of power exchange; it can be highly arousing, as long as it's about fulfilling her fantasies rather than only his. So, ladies, this chapter is all about making it work for you! Seriously, there are worse things than letting him worship the ground you walk on for a few hours – especially when it turns you both on.

Many men fantasise about having a strong, assertive woman take what she needs and make sexual demands. She demonstrates that she really, really wants him, so much so that she'll pin him down or tie him up and get what she needs. This woman is confident, sexy, powerful and knows what she wants. She may even be cruel or sadistic.

Female supremacy in the media

One of pop culture's first 'mansels in distress' was Major Steve Trevor from the 1970s *Wonder Woman* TV series. Wonder Woman, with her super-human strength and habit of carrying Steve out of burning buildings and crashed planes, was the archetypal dominant female. Another example is the vengeful Nancy Archer, with her towering mutated frame and 'giant desires', from the 1958 cult classic *Attack of the 50-Foot Woman.* In more recent years, its appeal continued in the TV show *Xena: Warrior Princess*. All three heroines share the attributes of the Femdom fantasy woman: height, beauty, confidence, strength and power.

Whereas Femdom is a common male fantasy, many women won't try it because the idea of being cruel and sadistic towards their lover isn't a turn on. When they are persuaded to try it, they do so reluctantly. As a result, the man often tries to 'top from the bottom' by telling his lady how to treat him. This defeats the purpose: the man doesn't get to relinquish control and the woman ends up feeling inadequate rather than empowered – which usually puts her off ever trying it again. The solution? Establish what you want from the experience, and dominate in *your* own way.

WHERE DO I START?

At this point you might be visualising some of the more embarrassing media portrayals of men pathetically grovelling at the feet of a latex-clad mistress. Whilst thigh-high boots are a popular fantasy, in reality what most men want more than anything is a woman who really **enjoys** dominating them. This is where your self-expression comes in.

Ask yourself: if you could get your lover to serve, please and pamper you in any way you like for a few hours, what would you want him to do? Make a detailed list. Here are some ideas.

- Treat you to a sensual all-over body massage as you instruct him on the pressure and technique that best pleases you

- Wear only an apron as he cooks your favourite meal, serves you, feeds you, then does the washing up

- Pop open a bottle of fine champagne and keep your glass topped up as you supervise him performing housework

- Worship your body from head to toe, kissing, nibbling, sucking or licking exactly as instructed

- Massage your feet when you arrive home after a tough day at work

- Run you a bath, slowly undress you and then bathe you, lovingly drying you off afterwards

- Go down on you on demand as you instruct him precisely on his technique: what pressure to apply, whether to use a finger, what action to use with his tongue, how to move his lips and how to eventually bring you to an intense orgasm – without you returning the favour

- Have sex with you according to your favourite angle, speed and position as you talk him through exactly what to do to make you climax

- Bring you breakfast in bed, along with several orgasms as he pleasures you through your morning toast

---

What kind of a man submits?

If you think submissive men are wimps you should meet my friend Christian, a successful, 6'2" muscle-bound Nordic blond with a penchant for being bound and flogged. There is absolutely nothing wimpy about this man. He's the type who in medieval times would have stood strong in the face of torture – a knight in shining armour, rescuing his lady and kneeling before her to do as she commands. There can be a great deal of strength in submission since many men like to be challenged and pushed to their physical or emotional limits.

CRACK THE WHIP

You'll need to spend some time well beforehand negotiating – communicating about likes, fantasies and limits for you both, as discussed earlier in this book. Be assertive about your own needs and limits as a Dominant. Start with activities you're genuinely happy to try and refuse to be pressured into going beyond that. Otherwise you risk putting yourself off the whole idea entirely.

When you're just finding your way, it's important for you to discover what you enjoy. Tell your lover that you're happy to dominate him but you'll be doing it your way. Make it clear that his role is to please you in the ways that matter to you. Ultimately he'll get more pleasure out of this too, since you'll be into it rather than just pretending. You'll also be able to go at your own pace.

This is a good time to lay out some ground rules:

- Down Boy! You're the one who decides when to initiate play – he's not allowed to pressure or nag you. You pick the time and the place, and you decide whether to give any notice or not.
- Play begins and ends when you decide.
- No topping from the bottom. This includes suggesting things or asking for more of something. You've already discussed your likes and dislikes, and if he wants to stop he can safeword.
- Tone down the grovelling. You may feel uncomfortable seeing your partner act pathetic, so ease into any humiliation play at a pace that suits you.
- Spend time after the scene cuddling and bonding. 'Aftercare', as it's known, is important, and Femdoms need reassurance and affection, too.

When cuddle time's over, talk about how you found the scene. What did he enjoy most? What did you enjoy most? Be specific. Men get a lot of pleasure from satisfying their lover, so this is your chance to praise him for a job well done. Keep it positive. Build each other's confidence by saying what you liked before discussing what you'd rather do differently next time.

Talk some more the next day, after you've had a chance to process everything. This is the time emotions such as guilt, shame or insecurity can emerge, so be honest about your feelings.

Finally: guys, give your partner plenty of affection, praise and encouragement in the days afterwards. Reassure your lady with a call, small gift or a visit to thank her for the wonderful experience she gave you.

What's in a name?

Scene names aren't necessary but they do make playtime special. They're a key part of the psychology of Domination/submission, since they highlight the power imbalance while you're playing. For example, you may wish to be called Mistress, Miss or Ma'am, and he may wish to be called Slave or Boy. You can also include protocol, such as insisting he responds 'Yes, Ma'am' when asked a question.

HOW TO PREPARE

If you've read the D/s chapter, you'll know that a successful scene hinges on good preparation. Plan each element in advance and have the toys you'll need to hand so you'll be able to relax and enjoy the moment when it arrives.

Think about what you'd like to do a couple of days prior and plan things that will excite and please you. Fancy the idea of giving him a surprise? Can you picture the look on his face when you order him to do something he hasn't considered? In the lead-up to the scene, have fun imagining how things will unfold.

Use the techniques in this book to build anticipation, perhaps texting him throughout the day or telling him how he is to prepare for your arrival. And when the time comes, demand exactly what you want, confidently and without apology. Forget "Can you top up my wine glass please?" – for tonight, it's "Top up my wine glass, Slave." Remember, for this time, you're the boss! There's no room for argument.

How to train your man

The great thing about regularly dominating your man is you're sexualising the behaviours that most please you – so don't be surprised when he suddenly starts volunteering to wash the dishes, clean the house or give you foot massages! These are now things he associates with pleasing you and feeling sexy, and men like to feel sexy.

This sexualisation of desired behaviour is known as 'male training' and some women get exceptionally good at it. A word of warning, however – many find that once they've 'trained' their man to perfection, they lose interest in him. You fell in love with him for a reason and it probably wasn't that he was a lap dog. So for most of us, it's best to keep Femdom an activity we indulge in for some fun, rather than making it a lifestyle choice.

THE ART OF FEMDOM

You'll find techniques and safety tips in the D/s chapter, but here are some things that as a woman you'll want to bear in mind.

- Don't just do this to make your lover happy. Find your own domination style and enjoy yourself. Wear what makes you feel sexy and do what you want to do, rather than comparing yourself to dominatrix characters you've seen on TV.

- Plan to do lots of the things you love. If you do something that feels good but find yourself confused about it, take time after the scene to reflect on it and talk about it.

- Stop whenever you like. Make sure you both have a safeword, and use it without hesitation if something isn't feeling right.
- Dominate only if you're in the mood.
- If he tries to top from the bottom, either demand an apology and 'punish' him by ordering him to do something you know he doesn't like, or call a halt to the scene entirely.
- There are no rules about how long a scene will last – it could be half an hour or a few hours.

A NOTE TO THE GUYS

Some of your fantasies might include more hardcore interests, such as latex catsuits, heavy bondage or extreme humiliation. My advice? Keep it to yourself for now.

This is about giving your lady the opportunity to get a feel for dominating you in her own way. Let her experience the thrill of being served, the rush of power that comes from controlling your pleasure, of being worshiped and having you at her mercy. She needs to enjoy the experience, which means taking things at a pace she's comfortable with.

Some men try to turn their partners into their fantasy Domme, but if you try that you're going to scare her off. Let her find her own way. She's a real-life woman with her own likes, dislikes, fantasies and desires, not that actress in the porn flick. If you want her to enjoy other forms of play, you'll need to have patience.

TEASE AND DENIAL

Aside from ordering him to serve you, what else can you do? Taking charge of how and when to let him orgasm can be a lot of fun: seeing him beg for release gives you a tremendous power rush and makes you feel desired. It's sexy, simple and involves no toys, and from his point of view it's exciting when a woman's confident enough to take control of his sexual release.

This sort of play can start hours or even days before the scene. Yes, there's a chance he could sneak off and masturbate, but why would he do that if he's serious about submitting to you? If he does, he'll probably confess, in which case you can decide to get him to start over or give him a punishment. Perhaps he can clean the oven, or sit and watch *The Notebook* with you?

Tease him mercilessly. Masturbate him in the morning without letting him come, titillate him with sexy messages when he's at work, call him and let him listen to you get yourself off, or order him to go down on you and make you come.

If you love intercourse, instruct him to penetrate you and bring you to climax without coming himself. When you're out and about, wear clothes you know he finds sexy and flirt outrageously with him, perhaps flashing him when no one's looking. Have fun with it!

When you finally let him come, he'll have to earn it. He might have to mow the lawn, fix your computer or take you shoe shopping. Previously mundane tasks will take on a whole new level of excitement when he knows he'll be granted or denied orgasm on the basis of his performance. Alternatively, set him sexual challenges, like making you come three times with different toys in one night.

Decide how you want him to orgasm as well. Would you like him to penetrate you slowly, in your favourite position, and at the angle and speed of your choice? Look into your eyes when he comes? Put on a show for you and masturbate himself to climax? Repeat a particular phrase as he comes, perhaps, "I will take out the garbage every day"? Don't be afraid to have fun with this!

If you'd rather confine your scene to one evening, you can tie him up and bring him close to orgasm over and over again without letting him come. By the time you finally grant him release, he'll do just about anything for you – and when he does come, it will be utterly earth-shaking.

HOW TO USE FEMDOM TO SYNC YOUR SEX DRIVES

If you have mismatched sex drives, playing with orgasm denial can help. If your drive is lower than his, denying him is part of the game, so you no longer need to worry about being pressured (and if he nags, you can invent punishments for that, too). If your sex drive is higher than his, you still win out, since you get to order him to bring you to orgasm whenever you like, however you like.

Remember, more than anything, domination is a mindset – one that can be embraced only so far as it's enjoyed. So do things on your terms, at your pace, and in your way. Here's an example of what's possible.

Revenge

Getting my own back feels so good. I've wrapped him from shoulders to feet in black pallet wrap, just the way I've watched him do it to me. He stands there, ankles so close together it's hard for him to balance. Totally mummified, unable to move a limb.

I give him a little push and see panic fill his eyes as he falls back onto the bed, unable to break his fall. He's taught me well.

But still he doesn't make a sound. His lips are clamped firmly together.

We've talked about this. Though he identifies as a Dominant, he has occasionally switched with someone he profoundly trusts. But he doesn't like to talk while he submits and prefers to have his identity concealed with a mask. This, he says, is the only way for him to allow himself to submit, since he can pretend he's someone else.

With me of course, he won't get off that easily. He's volunteered for me to dominate him and he knows I'm going to push his boundaries. Naturally.

"Try to get free," I order him, and he wriggles helplessly, his lips still clamped together.

"Is that all you can do? A big, strong man like you? Wriggle harder!"

He desperately tries to free himself. He's 6'2" and very fit but none of that counts right now.

I draw close to his face.

"I said, is that all you can do? Answer me."

His eyes look increasingly frantic but his lips stay sealed, so I slap him hard across the face. He gasps, finally letting out a moan.

"Do you want me to slap you again? Hmmm?"

When his voice comes out, it is unlike anything I have ever heard escape his lips: small, weak, compliant. "No Mistress," he mumbles.

"I can't hear you!" I position my hand, ready for another slap. He flinches.

"No Mistress!" he calls out.

"That's more like it." I smile sadistically. I'm really rather enjoying this.

I rip two holes in the pallet wrap and pinch his nipples.

"Ow!" he cries out.

"Say thank you," I command.

"Thank you, Mistress!"

"Thank you for what?" I ask, twisting a nipple again.

"Thank you for using me!"

"Good. Now, let's see how I can amuse myself with you. Oh, look at this! You've got a rock-hard cock, haven't you?"

His erection is pressed up tightly against the plastic, betraying his enjoyment. I rip a hole to free it and start to wank him. He lets out a moan, knowing he can't stop me. He is always totally in control but this time he knows I could make him come without his permission.

I reach behind me and pull out a surprise – it's a large kitchen knife. He gasps in horror. His trust in me fills me with a rush of love.

I know from observing him to use the back of the blade. Slowly, I trail the tip across his nipples, down his stomach and lower still.

"Don't move," I order him. He is so, so hard. He holds his breath and watches me closely, fascinated, as I gently trail the tip of the knife up to the end of his cock, being careful not to cut. When I stop, he breathes out, panting, moaning. I've barely touched him with the knife, but it's the trust in letting me do it that turns him on.

"Now let's turn you over," I say, rolling him onto his stomach. It's not easy; he's a big man. Once he's in position, I put a pillow under his head so he can look back at me.

"I think we need to show you just how dirty you are," I say, ripping a hole for his arse. His eyes are so vulnerable.

"Now let's put some lubrication on that tight little arsehole of yours, 'cause you're going to need it!"

He gasps in shock as I enter him with a finger, edging my way in.

"You like that, don't you?"

He says nothing, just moans, his lips clamped shut in shame.

"Do you want another slap? Answer me!"

"Yes Mistress, I love it!"

"What do you love, exactly?"

"I love you using my arsehole!"

His voice is weak, his eyes betray his humiliation.

"That's because you're a dirty boy, aren't you?"

"Yes Mistress! I'm a dirty little boy who loves to take it up the arse!"

"I think you need two fingers up there, don't you?"

"No Mistress – *please!*"

"Too late! Now take it you dirty boy!"

His face takes on a look I've never seen. He looks shocked, violated and aroused, all in one magnificent moment. I know how liberating it feels to totally let go and be brought this low and I'm enjoying showing him.

I edge out of him. "I'll be back in a moment," I say, "but while I'm gone I want you to struggle to see if you can get out."

I return a couple of minutes later and he's exhausted but still unable to free himself. I turn him onto his back again.

"I think it's time I used that rock-hard cock of yours to satisfy myself, don't you?"

"Yes Mistress."

"Because that's all it's there for, isn't it? It's just there for me to use and get myself off on."

"Yes Mistress!"

I lower myself onto his cock, grabbing him by the hair so he's compelled to look me in the eye as I force him into me.

"Struggle," I command and he obeys. "You can't get away, can you? Such a big, powerful man! Just look at you – you're being fucked and used by a little girl! And there's nothing you can do about it, is there?"

I slap his face hard.

"Ohhh!" His eyes are filled with desperation and arousal.

"That's right, take it," I say. I pull his hair and fuck him hard. "Mistress wants you to come for her pleasure. Now look at me when you come!" I order, and within seconds he is coming hard, a look of surrender on his face I've never seen before. He thrusts up, slamming himself into me as he lets out a cry, all the while holding my gaze.

As his orgasm fades, I pull back from his cock, holding the condom in place. I take it off with an evil smile. The expression on his face tells me he realises exactly what I'm about to do and can't believe how sadistic I am.

"Open wide," I command, and he has to comply. I spill the contents of the condom into his mouth.

"Now swallow like a good boy," I say. He gags on his own cum but he does as he's told.

I speak gently, affectionately, stroking his hair. "Now you know how it feels, hmmm? What do you say?"

"Thank you, Mistress," he replies, subdued and obedient.

Funnily enough, after that he never empties a condom into my mouth again. After all, what goes around, well, it cums around.

CHAPTER 13

ANAL ADVENTURES

Anal sex has officially gone mainstream. Just a few short years ago, it was a taboo interest that was illegal in much of the world. Today, however, it's a popular activity that 30 to 40% of the heterosexual population admit to indulging in. It could be said that anal sex is to this decade what oral sex was to the seventies.

But despite its popularity, it's still not readily discussed. For many of us there's a huge mental barrier as from the time we're toilet trained we've been taught the anus is the dirtiest part of the body. We were raised to see anal sex as unnatural, yet we're now told that scientifically the anus is without a doubt a prime erogenous zone.

The fact is there are thousands of sensitive nerve endings in and around it and it can feel fantastic when touched – in men because it's the only way to reach the prostate gland, and in women because of indirect G-spot and clitoral stimulation. And yes, that means some men and women can orgasm through anal stimulation alone.

Anal play, which involves any type of anal stimulation, is an intimate act: for many it requires a level of trust that's possible only with a long-term partner. In this chapter we'll explore it in its many forms, why you might enjoy it and how to go about it.

WHO'S INTO ANAL?

Giving and receiving anal play are normal activities that anyone of any gender, background or sexual orientation can enjoy. As one fan I talked to puts it, "the anus is an equal opportunity employer!"

However, as with all aspects of kinky play, it requires careful negotiation and above all consent. Pressuring someone to do something they don't want to do is just not on.

Take it like a man

Enjoying this type of stimulation doesn't make you gay. All men have a prostate gland that can be reached only through the anus, and it's common to be able to climax when it's massaged. Where you like to be touched depends on your nerve endings; which gender you prefer to have sex with depends on your sexual orientation. If you're a man, you probably enjoy getting a blow job, and so do most gay men – but that doesn't make you gay. So forget about how you might be perceived socially. If you and your partner like it, it's your choice and nobody else's business.

HOW DO I BRING THIS UP WITH MY LOVER?

Many women are put off anal sex because they've tried it and it was painful or they've heard from friends that it hurts. That's because those same nerve endings that make it feel great can also cause pain if subjected to bad technique.

For this reason, you need to know your stuff when you raise it with your lady. Reassure her that if she wants to try it you will take good care of her, and read this chapter thoroughly so you know how to make it a pleasurable experience for both of you.

According to best-selling sexpert Tracey Cox, "What puts most of us women off is having had the old 'Oops, I got the wrong hole' trick pulled on us. You 'accidentally' and eagerly thrusting into an unlubricated, unprepared anus hurts. And it's put plenty of women off for life. The second most likely thing to put us off is you asking for it, over and over and over again, which only makes us more determined not to do it."

So what's the best way to raise it?

"A playful suggestion that you'd like to try it – along with a 'you don't have to if you don't want to, but I'd at least like to try stimulating you with my fingers', will get you much further," says Cox. Emphasise that you'll be gentle, go slowly, and that if she doesn't like it you'll stop immediately.

I love being on the receiving end of anal play from my wife – it feels great, it's like another sex organ. She usually puts a butt plug inside me when we start to play and it stays in there till we finish having sex. The feeling as it rubs against my prostate is amazing, it takes the pleasure to another level. Anal play feels great and it has nothing to do with sexual orientation – after all, everybody has an anus! **– Joel**

COMMON MYTHS ABOUT ANAL PLAY

There are some scary rumours about about anal play, so before we look at how to do it I'd like to allay some of the fears you may have.

Is it painful?

Not if you're doing it with someone you feel comfortable enough to talk to, you use plenty of lube and you take it slowly. It's also important to be in a relaxed state of mind, have plenty of time on your hands and to be with a considerate, gentle lover who knows what they're doing.

Will my lover lose interest in conventional sex if we try anal?

It's highly unlikely. Most couples who indulge in anal sex tend to do so rarely, which is part of what makes it feel special.

But I'm of afraid of poo!

Faeces are stored in the colon; the rectum and anus are only passageways through which it travels, so it's unlikely you'll come into contact with it. But to ease your mind, go to the toilet beforehand if you need to and wash yourself inside and out in the shower. You can even shower together and wash each other as part of foreplay. If you're still worried, put a towel down beneath you and have wet wipes on hand.

Does anal sex cause haemorrhoids, constipation, diarrhoea or incontinence?

In a word, no.

SAFETY FIRST!

- Always wash your hands with a pH balanced antibacterial soap before play.

- Practise safe sex. This includes putting a condom over your penis and the toys you use. You may also want to use a pair of latex gloves during manual play, or a cut-up latex glove during oral play.

- Cut your fingernails short and file them down to avoid damaging the delicate anal tissue. Run your thumb around each nail and if you can feel one, file it down more to avoid cutting your partner.

- With any toy make sure it's smooth, flexible, clean, unbreakable and has a flared base so it can be easily removed.

- Use plenty of lube and keep re-applying.

- If you're switching from stimulating your lover's anus to her vagina, always wash your hands or change your condom first.

- Be gentle, ask for plenty of feedback and if something hurts, stop. Forcing things can do damage.

WHICH LUBE?

Some types of lubrication are made especially for anal play: they're thick and gloopy so they evaporate less quickly than the conventional kind. Choose a lube that is water-based, since oil-based ones tend to break down latex condoms and silicone-based lube doesn't work well with silicone toys. Something like Liquid Silk Lube is ideal: it's water-based and comes in a pump bottle so there's no mess. Steer well away from gels that contain anal desensitisers. These can numb you to the point where you're unaware of how much force you're taking, which can cause damage and pain later.

WHAT TYPES OF ANAL PLAY ARE THERE?

Anal fingering is a great place to start. Done carefully it feels very relaxing and can be as gentle as massaging the outside of the anus or gently probing. You may also wish to choose from the huge variety of toys made especially for anal play, which we'll look at later.

Analingus, known as 'rimming', entails stimulating the anus with your tongue. Anal sex involves penetration with the penis, and it can feel particularly intense for the man as the muscles of the anus are very narrow. Anal fisting requires intense trust, careful technique and plenty of experience. It's not something I'd advise when you're starting out.

ANAL PLAY – HOW TO DO IT

Go slow. Anal play is not best suited to a quickie, so make sure you have plenty of time on your hands. Many women are put off anal play of any kind because their lover rushed things and ended up hurting them. So be patient and understand that this is a process, not a one-off event.

Relax. Stress, including anxiety over whether it will hurt, causes the anal muscles to tighten, which makes penetration painful. So do everything you can to get your lover to relax in the way they enjoy best, whether that's running them a bath, giving them a massage or having a leisurely chat over a glass of wine.

Get them in the mood. Anal play feels best when you're really turned on. The more time you spend warming your lover up, the more they'll enjoy the experience. So do whatever it is they like you to do to get them in a peak state of arousal.

Use lots of lube. Unlike the vagina, the anus doesn't self-lubricate so you'll need to re-apply frequently.

Start on the outside. Trail your fingers teasingly across the perineum and gently massage the outside of the anus, giving your lover time to get used to the pleasurable, unusual sensations. When massaged sensually and carefully, the anus will open up without any need for force or pressure.

Penetrate with a finger. Go very slowly, edging a finger inside gradually. You can tease your lover by stopping and starting once it begins to feel good. In men, you'll want to focus on the prostate gland, located two centimetres inside the anus, which is so sensitive that some men can orgasm just from having it massaged.

Communicate. Make sure the partner being penetrated communicates throughout and gives plenty of feedback: how it feels, how fast to go, how deep, when to stop thrusting, and when to pull out.

Work your way up. There is no reason to go any further than this the first time. It's better to stop while things feel good rather than push things too far so your lover never wants to do it again. Get them used to the feeling of a finger inside them over time, then perhaps move up to a small butt plug or two fingers.

This takes time. It may take several occasions to bring your lover to the point where s/he is mentally and physically prepared and eager to move on to full anal sex, so take all the time you need. And if you only ever want to use a finger or a butt plug, that's OK, too.

Try adding other sensations. Some women enjoy vaginal penetration, clitoral or G-spot stimulation at the same time. Men may like their penis to be stroked or sucked at the same time as being penetrated anally. Experiment and see what works best.

NEWSFLASH: Forget what you see in porn flicks!

The rough anal sex you see in porn films really should come with a 'don't try this at home' label. Porn stars will wear butt plugs overnight before a shoot to stretch themselves and often use drugs and anaesthetic gel to numb the pain caused by hard thrusting.

The bottom line is, **do not** try to have anal sex the way you see it done in porn films. Doing so will result in painful sex and anal tearing and is a sure-fire way to put your partner off ever, ever wanting to try it again.

Pull out very slowly. Take your time and ease out very gently. Be guided by your lover as to how slow to go. They may well feel as though they need to visit the bathroom afterwards, and it will help them feel less shy about it if you suggest it.

Give lots of affection and support. Anal play is an incredibly intimate act and most people, especially those new to it, will need plenty of cuddles, validation and care afterwards. They may be facing feelings of shame, embarrassment or guilt. Be sure to call them the next day, too, to check they're doing OK.

ANAL TOYS

You can get just about every type of anal toy imaginable: vibrating ones, inflatable ones, anal beads, butt plugs, prostate stimulators, anal training kits, anal hooks – you name it! Some of them have rather amusing names like the 'Bend Over Boyfriend' and the 'Downunder' range.

Whatever you choose, make sure you use ONLY toys made specifically for anal stimulation. Also avoid toys containing phthalates, a group of rubber softening chemicals with harmful carcinogenic effects. Make sure anything you buy has 'phthalate free' on the packaging or in the online description.

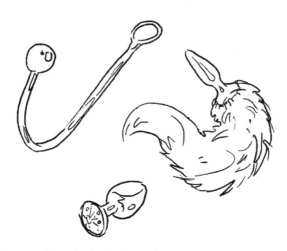

An anal hook, fluffy butt plug and anal jewellery

Here's a quick run-down of some of the more popular types of anal toys.

Butt plugs

These are diamond or bulb-shaped, with a flared base to prevent them from slipping out. The bulge in the middle keeps it in place and in men it stimulates the prostate. Butt plugs come in a variety of sizes and are good for beginners.

Anal dildos

A thin one is perfect if you're starting out. You can get them in silicone, glass or even steel – an interesting choice since you can pop it in the freezer or in a bowl of hot water beforehand for some interesting temperature play.

Anal jewellery

Forget lingerie – pretty and perverted, butt bling is daring, decorative and down-right cute! By far the most adventurous accessory out there, these opulent Swarovski crystal adorned plugs are available in a range of colours and sizes.

> *Sometimes, when I'm out with my husband, I'll surprise him by lifting my skirt to reveal that instead of the usual underwear there's a little sparkle between my cheeks. It always leads to a fun-filled night.* **– Alison**

Anal hooks

This stainless steel toy is perfect for couples who want to combine the joys of anal (or vaginal) play and rope. It has a ball on one end and a ring at the other end. Insert the ball into your lover's anus and thread some rope through the ring, then pull on the rope to move the steel ball inside them. Combining this with oral sex can be lots of fun, as you can see in the 'Hogtied' scene in the Bondage for Beginners chapter.

Fluffy butt plugs

These look extraordinarily cute, feel soft and sensuous to the touch and are available in an assortment of styles, from horse tails to fluffy fox tails. Most of them are faux fur so no animals were harmed in their making. As you can see in the following scene, they're perfect for role play.

Pet Play

I agreed to keep an open mind but I never thought I'd find myself here, on all fours, being transformed into his obedient puppy for the evening.

"No speaking," my Master commands, meeting my eyes. "Woof once for yes, twice for no. Understood?"

I woof once. I'm feeling more puppy-like every second – so playful and happy!

"Puppy needs a collar," he says, putting one around my neck and fastening the buckle. Collars always have a profound effect on me. Wearing one is the ultimate symbol of submission, of being owned. The leather feels lovely and snug around my neck.

"Now Puppy, Master has a present for you. Aren't you a lucky puppy!"

I can tell he's feeling playful, too.

He's holding a beautiful fluffy, fury tail with a large butt plug on the end. I gasp at how pretty it is. I know it will hurt when he puts it in me but I want that fluffy tail to be mine!

"Be brave now, Puppy. This will only hurt a little."

He lubes it up and puts it against my arse. I look at him and whine like a nervous little pup. He smiles, almost laughs, at the private joke between us.

I'm still whining as he lubes me up and pushes the tail into me. Pleasure and pain meld. It feels so big, but he's gentle.

"That's right Puppy. Such a good girl," he says, stroking my head as I whimper in discomfort.

"It's in all the way now – good Puppy!" He seems delighted. I'm overwhelmed with pleasure at seeing him so proud of me.

He pulls away to survey his handiwork, then smiles, satisfied.

"Let me hear your bells," he orders and obediently I shake about, making the bells clipped to my pert little nipples jingle.

"Woof!"

"Good puppy!" He really does look pleased.

And I'm overcome with excitability – I really do feel like his puppy! I waggle my tail for him, jingle my bells and woof. I roll over for him to tickle my tummy, paws in the air, whining.

He laughs. "Puppy's feeling playful!"

I woof once. Oh I am so proud of my tail, my beautiful, fluffy, furry tail! Reading my mind, he comes around and strokes it. Wow, the sensation is incredible!

He attaches a leash to my collar. "It's time to take puppy for a walk," he says.

I proudly walk on all fours, wagging my beloved tail as he leads me around the room.

"Sit!" he orders as we get to the kitchen. I obediently kneel, paws in front.

"Now stay," he orders, putting the leather handle of the leash between my teeth.

I whine eagerly as I see him bring out the take-away food. He smiles.

"A plate for Master," he says, dishing the food out, "and a bowl for Puppy."

I am instantly soaking wet.

He walks me back to the lounge and orders me to sit. I whine, looking eagerly at the food.

"Is Puppy hungry?" he asks.

"Woof!"

He takes a fork full of Thai noodles and feeds me, one mouthful after another, until I am full. I'm overcome by the kindness of my master. When he treats me as his pet it is such an act of thoughtfulness and care. It would be impossible for us to demonstrate such playful affection any other way.

"Now fetch Master his wine."

I trot over obediently to his wine glass but I am really in role, and when I get to it I stand there on all fours, confused, looking back and forth between him and the wine.

"You can use your paw," he laughs.

"Woof!" I reply, and bring his wine back to him. He takes a long sip.

I'm looking at his cock.

"Would Puppy like a treat?"

"Woof!"

He pulls on my leash, bringing my face close to his glorious cock. It's so, so hard.

"Put Master's cock in your mouth then, Puppy," he commands.

I feel so grateful to be given my treat! I wag my tail and woof, then lean in to take him deep in my mouth. He strokes my hair gently, groaning.

"Goooood puppy," he says, his cock deep in my mouth. I whine in response. He knows how grateful I am.

He leans back, sipping on his wine as I suck him. Then he draws out of my mouth and walks round to kneel behind me.

"I think it's time Master fucked you in that tight little puppy-cunt."

"Woof!"

"Let's just move this tail aside,"

"Woof!"

The tail feels soft against my skin as he lifts it up, penetrating my wet pussy. I stifle a laugh. I know this is his idea of a joke: we're doing it doggy-style.

PART III
GETTING GEARED UP

Toys aren't just for kids – we all like to play. I never understand why lovers buy each other flowers, which soon wilt, or the same boring aftershave, when they could give gifts that bring them both hours of entertainment, intimacy and orgasms.

The couple that plays together stays together, so in this chapter you'll discover all sorts of toys to experiment with – many of which I'll bet you didn't even know you had.

CHAPTER 14

THE FREE SEX TOYS ALL AROUND YOUR HOME

Household items can be re-purposed for all sorts of frisky functions with a little creative thinking. This chapter is by no means exhaustive but it should inspire you to look at the items in your home in a new light.

Kitchen

Get your mitts on those cold metal kitchen utensils – even forks and spoons dragged across skin can feel wonderful. Heighten the sensation by putting them in the freezer for a while before play, or heating them up in a warm bowl of water. And while you're at it, fill that ice tray up – ice is a classic for all sorts of temperature play.

Blindfold your lover and use food from the fridge. Ice cream, olives, honey – anything you like can be fed to them or licked off them.

For spanking, try using a wooden spoon or spatula. Even the humble rubber egg poacher can be used to cup a man's testicles for a very unusual massage, and a pastry brush drawn across the skin can feel divine.

Knives can be powerfully erotic but require careful handling, as you don't want to break the skin. Choose a fairly blunt knife, turn it over and trail the back of the tip gently across your lover's back, chest, thighs or legs for an emotionally charged experience.

A long kitchen table makes perfect bondage furniture, especially with a couple of cushions on top to make it more comfortable. Either tie your lover to it spread-eagle or put them on their tummy and hogtie them.

Kitchen chairs are usually armless so they're ideal for over-the-knee spanking. You can also tie your lover to one, perhaps for an interrogation role play.

Laundry

Clamp clothes pegs to different parts of the body like nipples, arms or thighs. Plastic ones usually have a firmer bite than wooden ones. The longer you leave them there, the more intense the sensation will be when you remove them.

A feather duster is perfect for dragging across your lover's skin when they're tied and feels great alternated with sandpaper or a sound spanking. Your mop can be used as an improvised spreader bar if you attach ankle cuffs to it.

Lounge and dining room

Hogtying your lover on a coffee table puts them at the perfect height for you to penetrate their mouth if you kneel down. Again, be sure to put cushions on the coffee table to make it comfortable, and please don't try this with a glass table!

You can attach a sex swing to a door; and candles, chillout music and incense or essential oils all help create atmosphere.

Study

You can use certain types of paperwork clips as nipple clamps. A swivel chair is perfect for a little tie and tease, and you can even blindfold your lover and spin them round.

Your study is, of course, the perfect place for a boss/ secretary role play. Bending your lover over the desk for a spanking is especially fun – watch the film *Secretary* if you need inspiration.

Use biro pens to draw or write all over your lover's naked body. The sensation is quite unusual, and if your lover is blindfolded you can write messages for them to discover once the scene is over.

Bedroom

Stockings can bunch up painfully if you use them to tie wrists, but used in a different way they are a very versatile bondage tool. Cut the legs off several pairs of old stockings, put your lover's hands behind their back and slide one leg over both their arms. Several layers of this creates a stretchy home-made arm binder, restraining them so that when you lift their hands they're forced to bend over. You can do the same thing to bind their legs together.

Dive into your wardrobe and hunt out scarfs, men's ties or pillowcases for blindfolds, and perhaps a belt for some impact play. Chances are you have all manner of sexy clothes to dress up in, too: high heels, stockings and lingerie are obvious choices. A large mirror is ideal for watching each other; after all, some positions don't allow for eye contact.

You can use a hairbrush in many ways. The obvious one is as a spanking implement, or you can drag it across the skin for sensation play. Tell your lover to lie on their stomach as you straddle them and slowly sweep the bristles across their shoulders, all the way down to their buttocks and the backs of their thighs. This feels quite incredible.

Bobby pins are handy, too. Use the pointy end to draw large circles around your lover's nipples, getting smaller and smaller until you eventually touch them. As the anticipation builds, use the bobby pin as an improvised nipple clamp. Because you've slowly built the sensation, the pinching feels intensely pleasurable.

Bathroom

Dental floss is ideal for nipple bondage: tie a slipknot in it and pull it tightly around your lover's nipple.

You can use a shaving brush, makeup brush or even a toothbrush for sensation play. Alternating between a stiff and a soft brush on areas like breasts, nipples and inner thighs feels divine.

Mouthwash adds another dimension to oral sex. Just swish some around your mouth beforehand and the menthol creates an interesting tingly sensation.

Use an electric toothbrush as an improvised vibrator by pressing it to the clitoris. And then, of course, there's the bath and shower. Bathe your lover as part of a Domination/submission act of service or wash them in the shower and dry them off afterwards. As lots of women know, a showerhead on the massage setting can bring you to orgasm.

Garage or shed

A plastic scraper for clearing ice from a car windshield makes a good paddle. The garage is also the place to find rope, cable ties (wide ones only please) and perhaps even pallet wrap for bondage. You can use sandpaper and paintbrushes for sensation play.

For sensory deprivation scenes, nothing cuts out sound better than a pair of ear muffs. You can also use a flashlight to explore your lover's body in the dark, or for a medical or interrogation role play.

CHAPTER 15

CREATE YOUR OWN SEX TOY KIT

Sex toys around your house are all very well but as any tradesman will tell you, you need the right tool for the job. Purpose-made toys bring hours of frisky fun, but where do you start?

Even with just the basic toys in the starter kit below, you'll be able to do many of the activities in this book. But we can all dream, so I've added some more ideas for those of you who want to take things up a notch or two.

Yes, I list a lot of sex toys here – and finding the cheapest place to buy them online can be a drag. So remember, to save you the hassle I've compiled a definitive list of all the toys listed in this book, by chapter – and where to buy them at great prices from reliable suppliers, who ship their items in discreet packaging.

Access my free 'Secret Sex Toy Guide' at http://thekinkysexbook.com/secret-sex-toys/.

THE STARTER KIT

Hitachi Magic Wand: The Rolls-Royce of vibrators. Accept no substitutes.

Lube: Don't come home without it.

Blindfold: Another essential item.

Nipple clamps: From the humble clothes peg to titillating tweezer clamps.

Lelo's Lyla 2 remote control bullet vibrator: Hands-free public orgasms. Oh God yes!

Durex's vibrating rubber cock ring: Why should the ladies have all the fun?

Under bed bondage kit with buckle-up cuffs: Fit for a king – or queen, double or twin.

Hogtie kit: For restraining your lover quickly and easily.

Buckle-up wrist and ankle cuffs: No knots necessary. Makes bondage a snap.

Rope: Nylon, jute, cotton, hemp, silk: each has its own sensation.

Collar and leash: And while you're there...

Collar and Leash

Crop: Discipline with just a flick of the wrist.

10mm-wide cable ties: Hit your local hardware store for these.

Vetrap (pronounced Vet-rap): Available from pet shops or online. Didn't think you'd be headed to the pet shop, did you?

Clothes: High heels, fireman's hats, hold-ups, leather trousers, fishnets, lingerie, power suits, etc.

Candles for hot wax: Use in power play, not just power failures.

THE INDULGENCE KIT

Butt plugs: Jewelled butt bling, fluffy-tailed, inflatable, vibrating, chrome...

Sex sling: Hang around in comfort.

Sex Sling

Latex arm binder: Keeps arms behind your back, and hands away from mischief.

Hood: Blocks out sight and sound for maximum touch sensation.

Spreader bar: A rigid metal rail with ankle cuffs to keep legs apart.

Posture collar: For oral mounting. Hold your head high, like it or not!

Metal anal hook: Attach to rope for hands-free anal or vaginal stimulation.

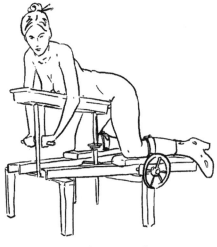

Spanking Bench

Floggers: Available in suede for soft sensations or hard leather for stingy impact.

KinkLab's Neon Wand: Uses static electricity for tingles all over.

Bondage sack: You'll be snug as a bug in a rug, with strategically placed access points for various nefarious purposes.

Role play outfits and accessories: Perhaps a stethoscope for medical play or handcuffs for an interrogation scene.

Latex catsuits and latex sheets: Just add lots of lube for slippy, slidey latex sex.

Electro play kit, with insertables and rubber cock loops: The only thing that will still shock you after reading this book!

IN YOUR DREAMS

Suspension point: Hangs from a support beam. Fit your fantasy home with one in every room.

Saint Andrew's Cross

Spanking bench: Clear a fair amount of space for this one and tell the in-laws it's gym equipment.

Saint Andrew's Cross: A two-metre-high piece of furniture for binding your lover spread-eagle in a standing position. A bit harder to explain to the in-laws.

Cage

Cage: For containing those animal urges. Tease your lover through the bars.

Bondage bed: For sleepless nights spent turning and, er, tossing.

EPILOGUE
....

WHERE TO FROM HERE?

We've come a long way, Baby. Just a few short decades ago, even oral sex was frowned upon because it was non-procreational.

The internet has exposed us to greater sexual variety than we could ever have imagined. We expect more from our sex lives than at any other time in history, yet there's little information on how to use novelty and experimentation to heighten desire and develop fulfilling, committed relationships.

Until now. With the information in this book, you're now prepared to build the kind of sexually exciting relationship many only dream of. Faced with that previously intimidating nine-course meal, you'll be confident about exactly which cutlery to use – and can probably think of plenty of other purposes for those seemingly innocent knives, forks and spoons!

Sex is the only skill that's assumed to come naturally to us with no need for study, practice or discussion. But it doesn't. I hope that by reading this book, you've experienced as significant a shift in perspective as I did when I realised this truth.

The great news is that you now know the essential ingredients to a fun, vibrant, explorative sexual connection, and you're ready to start playing. So grab your nipple clamps, lube your latex and go have some kinky fun!

ABOUT JESSICA HOWE

Swedish-born Australian author Jessica Howe has been many things: journalist, wedding book writer, consultant who whipped CEOs into shape, waitress who spilled soup into people's laps. All, quite remarkably, without kinky intentions.

Jessica migrated to England at the age of three and grew up in a small village near Windsor. She spent her teens at a very proper single-sex boarding school, then studied history at The University of Birmingham where, on her third day, she met the man she would marry.

On graduating she flirted with journalism, toyed with TV, then settled into consulting, a career which took her all over Europe coaching senior executives in some of the world's largest companies. Craving fresh challenges she traded the cold British weather for the balmy climes of Australia, where she became a citizen.

Her inspiration for *Kinky Sex – the Secret to Long-term Desire* came at a crossroads in her life when her marriage collapsed after fourteen years. It is the culmination of seven years she spent on both sides of the globe following the break-up, in a quest to answer the question "How is long-term desire possible?" Solving that riddle became her obsession, since she knew only the answer could restore her faith in relationships.

And so it did. So she waved goodbye to her trouser suits, quit her sensible job and resolved to share the secrets she'd discovered. Her books and online courses now help singles all over the world to find sexually compatible partners, and couples to reverse the slow, painful decline into the wasteland of sexless relationships.

Despite her forthright writing style and confident demeanor Jessica is at heart a romantic, one-guy girl who is even a little shy. She has been referred to by more than one journalist as 'the girl next door who likes to be tied up'.

She currently lives in Sydney, Australia, but frequently travels internationally.

Want to dive deeper?

Join the Kinky Sex Book community for secret kinky tips, special member-only offers and to ask me questions directly. Just go to www.thekinkysexbook.com and click on 'Join the Community'. See you there!

Made in the USA
Lexington, KY
14 February 2014